Radio Programming:
Tactics and Strategy

Broadcast & Cable Series
Series Editor: Donald V. West, Editor/Senior Vice-president,
  Broadcasting & Cable

Radio Programming Tactics and Strategy

Eric G. Norberg

Focal Press

An Imprint of Elsevier

Boston   Oxford   Johannesburg   Melbourne
New Delhi   Singapore

Focal Press

An Imprint of Elsevier

Copyright © 1996 All rights reserved.

Permissions may be sought directly from Elsevier's Science and Technology Rights Department in Oxford, UK. Phone: (44) 1865 843830, Fax: (44) 1865 853333, e-mail: permissions@elsevier.co.uk. You may also complete your request on-line via the Elsevier homepage: http://www.elsevier.com by selecting "Customer Support" and then "Obtaining Permissions".

Library of Congress Cataloging-in-Publication Data
Norberg, Eric G.
 Radio programming: tactics and strategy / by Eric G. Norberg.
  p. cm.—(Broadcasting & cable series)
 Includes index.
 ISBN 0-240-80234-9 (pbk.)
 1. Radio programs—Planning. I. Title. II. Series.
PN1991. 55. N67   1996   95-50768
791. 44'0236—dc20   CIP

British Library Cataloguing-in-Publication Data
A catalogue record for this book is available from the British Library.

The publisher offers discounts on bulk orders of this book.
For information, please contact:
Manager of Special Sales
Butterworth-Heinemann
225 Wildwood Avenue
Woburn, MA 01801-2041
Tel: 781-904-2500
Fax: 781-904-2620
For information on all Butterworth-Heinemann publications
available, contact our World Wide Web home page at:
http://www.bh.com

Transferred to Digital Printing 2007

To my wife, friend, assistant, and partner,
Jane Kenney-Norberg

Contents

Preface

As a student, teacher, writer, and, especially, practitioner of radio from 1960 to the present, I've read many books on modern radio programming. Many have seemed interesting and well written, but to date every book I've read has presented techniques of programming radio stations that amount to "how I do it." Many of the points made are useful and will work when applied, but generally they must be applied as the author dictates in order to work.

My purpose in writing this book is to present the principles by which modern radio programming is constructed. Although I do give examples to clarify points, generally speaking I'm dealing with underlying principles only, and I encourage you to find your own unique approach using these principles. For programmers who are not yet confident enough in their skills to program contrary to the way that everybody else is doing it, these principles will help you understand why the stations you are copying do succeed. It will also help you grasp which of their techniques might not be useful for you to use and which may be relevant to your own market situation.

Radio's role in our culture is unique, and unless the fundamentals of what make it so are explored and understood, we cannot succeed with it in the future. This, then, is the first radio programming handbook I'm aware of that actually deals with radio programming tactics—a complete guide to the strategies underlying the creation of the magic that allows radio to be the most powerful medium of communication ever invented.

Two factors combine to create radio's power. The first is that radio can be "consumed" while the listener is doing something else. All other forms of mass communication require the consumer's focused attention before communication can occur. Radio has evolved into a personal companion—a soundtrack accompaniment to our lives—as a result of this unique characteristic.

The second trait of radio that contributes to its power is that the technology by which it reaches the listener is uniquely invisible. When we read, we absorb the author's thoughts, but we are still aware that we are scanning symbols on a page. When we watch television or a movie, we can get lost in a good story or follow a well-articulated thought, but we are never unaware that we are watching a reproduction on a screen. In each case, the means of communication itself forms a subtle barrier between us and the author or participants. When we listen to radio, however, the original voice, the music as it was created, reaches us through transparent technology. We do not hear the "sound" of the loudspeaker other than as pure sound. This allows us to respond in a more fundamentally personal way to what we hear than is possible with any other form of communication, in all of which the medium itself always becomes part of the message.

Further amplifying radio's power is something called the "transactional analysis principle." I once read a best-selling book about this called *Born to Win*. To summarize the essence of it for our discussion, I can distill it to this: People respond to us as we present ourselves to them. People react to us in the same way we act toward them. This is true in any context, but in radio this principle is uniquely effective because when others see us, part of the way we present ourselves to them includes such irrelevancies as what we look like, what we've chosen to wear, an unnoticed food stain on our sleeve, and the complexities of body language. In radio, all of these are absent, and all that's left of us is our voice. Through training, practice, and attitude, we are able to control fully the way our voice touches listeners. In radio, the rapport between us and our listeners can be complete—and intense.

A number of years ago, in a *TV Guide* article, a university professor said that two-thirds of all spoken communication is nonverbal. At first, I rejected this idea because it seemed to suggest that television is much more effective at communicating than radio, which I knew to be untrue. (Actually, the reverse is the case.) However, after a little thought, I realized what the man really meant, and I had to agree with him. His point was that 70 percent of all communication is other than simply the words spoken, and that is true. The way we say them, the attitude we project, is what really communicates what the words are saying. Because of the transparency of the medium, radio can communicate in this way far better than all other media.

When we speak on the radio, we are speaking intimately to just one person. If we want that person to relate to us, to care who he or she is listening to, to pay attention to what we say, and to act on it, we must drop our own personal defenses and relate to our listener as we would to a close friend. Personality, in radio, consists of no more than this, and over the years, I have come to understand that everybody is capable of being a personality. The tough part for many people is realizing that—whatever their own "secret demons"—they are nonetheless just like everyone else, and they are likable people. Therefore, we must let the listener experience us as we really are.

The human being, a live person, is the essence of radio, and this will be as true in the future as it is today and has always been. Television is evolving in interesting ways as the computer comes closer to merging with it. As the television audience fragments, it becomes harder for local stations to make money in the expensive business of TV. Direct broadcast satellite and cable-delivered systems create more and more nationwide cable networks to respond to the need for low-cost-per-viewer programming.

For radio, though, the essence remains the relatable (local) person on the air, and this requires no extraordinary costs. As TV becomes more and more "wired in," radio—the truly wireless, portable companion—has, if anything, an even brighter future than its remarkable past.

Radio must play to its strengths to realize this future. In the years to come, there will be more and more direct-from-satellite and cable-delivered radio services, and there will be more audio services consisting of music without voice. Radio, in the sense addressed in this book, will survive and prosper only by retaining its permanent advantages. It must avoid, as much as possible, full automation and satellite-delivered programming, both of which tend to lower this lucrative kind of localized radio to the glossy impersonality of TV and other media.

After all, what's the real difference to the listener between a satellite-delivered format coming from a local station and the same format coming straight from a direct-broadcast satellite? Mostly, just local commercials and perhaps a little wire-service news. That's not a very meaningful difference. The satellite format providers are well positioned to cut the local stations that relay their programs right out of the loop when the time seems right.

Thus there are two elements that radio stations must retain if they are to survive and prosper—and these are the elements that listeners value most in radio anyway: localism and human contact. We'll talk more about these as we travel together through this book.

Acknowledgments

I'd like to acknowledge some of the people who have been mentors to me at critical moments in my radio career and thus have had a definite impact on this book:

Ken Warren

Galyn "Doc" Hammond

Don Hofmann

Mark Blinoff

Richard Kale

Bill Gavin

Special thanks to programmer and consultant Paul Drew for his insightful and critical reading of the initial manuscript.

The Basic Principles of Radio Programming

The Station versus the Programs

From the twenties to the mid-fifties, radio was a program-oriented medium. Listeners tuned in programs, and which station (or even which network) broadcast them was relatively unimportant. Television snatched away this function in the fifties, and at first, amid steep audience declines, it appeared that radio—the broadcast medium that didn't have pictures—had been made irrelevant by video. The funeral was premature.

The first step toward modern format-oriented radio occurred in Omaha, Nebraska. According to legend, Todd Storz was hunting for something profitable to do with his daytime radio station, KOWH. He was talking it over with colleague Bill Stewart in a bar when they noticed that customers played the same songs over and over again on the bar's jukebox. Storz and Stewart reasoned that if they limited the station's music playlist to the songs that drew the most plays in juke-boxes and played them repeatedly, KOWH would draw an audience. It did. The daytime-only station rapidly drew audience shares of well over 50 percent.

Cut to Dallas, Texas. Gordon McLendon had already had some real success in radio. He had formed the national Liberty Network to broadcast baseball "games of the week," but the major-league baseball teams refused to grant him the rights to broadcast their games. He solved this problem by arranging to get pitch-by-pitch, play-by-play telegraph reports on selected games from an observer posted in the stands. From these reports, he re-created the games in his Texas studio, using sound effects and his own sense of drama. Most listeners never realized that "the old Scotchman" who brought them the games was neither old nor present at any of the games.

The Liberty Network was history by the mid-fifties, and McLendon by then was in charge of KLIF in Dallas, a minor independent AM radio station owned by his father. He was intrigued by reports of what KOWH was doing in Omaha, and after checking it out, he installed his version at KLIF. Thus Top 40 was born—as was all modern radio formatting. Legendary stations—WABC, WLS, WQAM, WINS, KOMA, KFWB, KRLA, WMGM, CKLW, KYA, KFRC, WCFL, KJR, KHJ, WMCA, and many others—refined it.

What McLendon added to the Storz-Stewart concept was a sense of showmanship and the understanding that to succeed, the new Top 40 format had to define the cutting edge of the youth popular culture. Young people have always defined the forward edge of the pop culture; this was as true back in the big-band era as it is today. Adults eventually adopt what started out as an unsettling youth phenomenon (in music, fashion, consumer culture, everything), whereupon the young people move on, always seeking to define themselves in ways that differentiate them not only from their parents, but also from the generation that immediately preceded them. Top 40 radio thus needed to concentrate on the current hits, played over and over, because the current hits—established by sales and requests—define the group that defines itself by the music, which is the teens, the most active group buying hit records and calling request lines. It is true that only the real "activists" of the teen culture are doing most of the buying and requesting, but the youth culture is created by those activists, so it is quite legitimate to use that data to program a Top 40 station.

Top 40 tends to draw large adult audiences for two reasons. First, many of those adults are parents of the teens (or subteens) who turn the station on. Second, many adults like to feel that they are still in tune with the youth culture. Because many of those buying "spins" on the Omaha jukeboxes were adults, they too valued the ease and comfort of getting what they wanted when they wanted it. So the basic "format radio" principle was applicable, with modifications, to adults too—and McLendon was smart enough to realize that, although it was not until 1959 that competitive circumstances led him to develop format radio in other directions—first at KABL, Oakland-San Francisco, where he developed the successful package with harps and poetry for the Beautiful Music format; and later in Los Angeles via XETRA, Tijuana, Mexico, with the first solidly successful All-News format.

The show business element that McLendon brought to format radio included the development of high-profile personalities to whom the core audience could relate and the use of stylized format elements, such as outrageous stunts and intriguing on-air contests. His imaginative promotions included running commercials for imaginary services, to tweak the listeners! Courtesy of Dave Verdery at KBIG in Los Angeles, who worked for McLendon, here's a portion of a memo by Gordon about this unusual promotional idea:

> *Along with station promos, exotics are your major cause of listener talk. These should be scheduled at least once every three hours throughout the day. The best exotics seem to be those which are completely incongruous with the idea, i.e., advertising the Brooklyn Ferry in San Francisco. Good sources for exotics are distant areas, selling products not normally sold in this area, advertising something completely foreign to the general thought, etc. All exotics should be played perfectly straight; they should never be done live. All should be perfectly produced and recorded. They have a tendency to annoy many people and you will receive quite a few complaints. Ignore them. Exotic commercials are almost the backbone of this type of operation. It is believed they are second only to the actual music policy of KABL's success.*

Many of those who listened to KLIF and its many imitators in the late fifties and early sixties remember the stations as rock-and-roll radio. However, the published Top 40 playlists show that many of the records played were not rock and roll at all. Some songs were ballads from artists like Frank Sinatra, Tony Bennett, Doris Day, and Rosemary Clooney. Bennett's "I Left My Heart in San Francisco" was a Top 40 hit in the fall of 1962.

There are always hit records that originate in older pop styles but that nonetheless appeal to the young and are legitimately part of the cutting edge of the pop culture. Hit radio stations in later decades all too often forgot that. They arbitrarily rejected any then-current pop hit records not seen as mainstream youth records, which reduced their station's appeal to all components of their audience. The only justification for the wide variety that has characterized successful Top 40 radio is that all these records are united by being current hits. That free-ranging variety has always been the essence of Top 40's wide demographic appeal.

To Gordon McLendon, then, we must award credit for originating much of what radio became in the latter half of the twentieth century. Stations learned that attracting audiences begins with consistency. These principles have been refined over the years by such outstanding programmers and consultants as Mike Joseph, Bill Gavin, Paul Drew, Kent Burkhart, Lee Abrams, Bill Stewart, George Burns, Rick Sklar, and many others. Once radio had been reinvented as an ongoing, lifestyle-oriented audio accompaniment, it became station-oriented instead of program-oriented. People today choose stations to listen to based on their own perceptions of what kind of service the station will offer, rather than on any specific program.

There is one exception to this, though. Play-by-play sports coverage is perceived as a program. As I have had plenty of opportunity to observe and research in my career, listeners will tune to whatever station they must to hear that "program." Afterward, they return to the stations to which they usually listen. This creates unforeseen problems for stations that use sports to draw casual listeners whom they hope to convert to regular listeners. This is discussed in more detail in the next chapter.

The Importance of Consistency

Today, successful stations devote themselves consistently to one type of programming. This programming generally consists of a mixture of compatible elements, such as newscasts, commercials, and air personalities. The principle of consistency can be refined as follows: Successful programming consists of fulfilling listener expectations, and listener expectations are based mostly on what the station has done in the past. This refinement makes clear what a programmer must do to maximize the success of a radio station. A station must be consistent with what it has done in the past to reinforce listener expectations.

To succeed as a program director, you must be able to hear your station, and radio in general, from the perspective of the listener. You'll have to get into the listener's head—a listener who is much less preoccupied with radio than you are—to understand how the audience actually perceives your station and the competition.

If your station matches listener expectations when they tune in, they feel rewarded, and the behavior of tuning in your station more often and listening longer is reinforced. If your station fails to match listener expectations, the audience's perception of your station is weakened, and they will tune in less often and listen for shorter intervals each time.

What about ratings, which are discussed in much greater depth in Chapter 8? When a station does not meet listener expectations, the weekly cumulative audience will hold up quite well for a considerable period of time, as listeners tune in from time to time, hoping that the station will again be as they expect it to be. However, the average quarter hour share, which is based on the average listening span, will show a downward trend. In this case, all that's necessary is to realign the station to listener expectations. In many cases, though, station management reacts by changing the format in the hope of building a bigger but different audience for a new service—thus destroying the expectations of the existing audience altogether. Building a new audience is almost always harder than "fixing" an existing station that already has an established audience.

In the context of listener expectations, exactly what a station is doing at any given instant is almost irrelevant to the established image of the station. This point hit me one day when one of my on-air personalities at KEX in Portland, Oregon, where I was the program director at the time, stopped by my office with an observation that puzzled him. He had been at a laundromat and noticed that the radio on the shelf there was not tuned to Adult Contemporary KEX as it usually was, but instead had been turned to Top 40 KGW. As he proceeded with his laundry, the manager of the laundry popped out of her office, looked around suspiciously, asked who had changed the radio, and retuned the receiver to KEX. Then she visibly relaxed and went back into her office. What puzzled the deejay was that, at that moment, both stations were playing the same song. The manager's relief at retuning her favorite station could not have been based on the music that the two stations were actually broadcasting when she changed the station. Actually, the manager's rejection of KGW and her preference for KEX were based on her perception of what each station represented—and what sort of music she expected to hear next on each. What a station is playing right now can be almost irrelevant to the listener's image, and thus expectations, of the station.

There is another dimension to listener expectations—one that probably played a major part in the laundry manager's reaction. As noted earlier, with modern formatting, radio became a lifestyle medium. As a result, listeners choose their favorite station at least partly because it seems to reflect them—their tastes, their values, their very selves. It's a "cultural mirror" for them, in that respect—a touchstone by which they define themselves and with which they keep in touch with the elements of their culture.

This special role of radio is most obvious in ethnic broadcasting, but it's important for all listener segments, which is why demographics—the age groups into which ratings are customarily divided—are quite inadequate to define radio audiences. Adult contemporary pop music stations, oldies stations, country music stations, classic rock stations, and jazz stations generally compete for the same demographics, but they reach very different audiences in terms of lifestyle.

The role of radio as a cultural mirror motivates listeners to use a station as a "soundtrack" for their lives, and it explains why people get so enraged when "their station" changes format. After all, it's a bit like looking into the mirror and seeing a stranger looking back at you. A format change seems to be a rejection of the listener's values—and even his or her identity. Radio people sometimes underestimate the important role our stations play in people's lives. Just answer the phones after a format change!

Radio formatting once was a much simpler job than it is now; even big markets had relatively few radio stations with significant audiences, and all were on the AM band. (FM stations were not even included in most ratings until the mid-sixties; measurable FM audiences were usually lumped into the "miscellaneous" category until then, except by the Hooper Rating service.) By the eighties, when FM stations commonly drew audiences larger than the AM stations did, there was such a large choice of stations in most areas that niche programming became the rule, and most AM and FM stations began catering to small segments of the available audience.

Up until the seventies, even second-rate stations could expect to get a 5 percent or larger share of the audience in a crowded market. By the eighties, even leading stations in competitive markets were fighting it out for shares of less than 3 percent of the audience. This does not mean that it's pointless to try to serve a broad "mass" audience—even moderate success in doing so could easily result in a profitable audience share—but it does require that a programmer have an ever clearer idea of how listeners perceive his or her radio station.

At this point let me recommend a book to you—a book that every program director, every general manager, and every sales manager should read and keep handy: *Positioning: The Battle for Your Mind*, by Al Reis and Jack Trout (New York: McGraw-Hill, 1981). Although it was published in 1981 and some of its examples are out-of-date, it's still in print and it remains the definitive work on modern communication. The central premise of the book is that people perceive new things by relating them to the things they already know. For example, consider these terms: *horseless carriage, tubeless tire, offtrack betting, unleaded gasoline*. In addition, top-of-mind awareness, arising from how people mentally rank the alternatives in each product category, determines expectations and consumption patterns.

The authors cite the brilliant positioning of 7-Up against the dominant soft drink as "the un-cola," moving 7-Up from its own product category to the number three position in the "cola" category behind Coca-Cola and Pepsi. Though most examples in the book are drawn from advertising, the underlying theme is communicating in an overcommunicated world, and radio is very definitely in the communication business. Read the book and understand its lessons if you hope to win the radio wars.

FM versus AM

Statistically, there is an approximately equal chance that you, as a radio programmer, will be assigned the programming of an AM or FM station; there's roughly five thousand of each licensed for commercial broadcasting in the United States. The evolution of AM and FM broadcasting services in the United States has led to two different sets of listener expectations for the two bands, and amazingly few radio people realize that this must be clearly understood and taken into consideration to maximize success on each band.

The distinction between listener expectations of AM and FM stations has proved quite durable over the last twenty-five years. Yet broadcasters today often try to program mainstream formats on AM as they do on FM, and when it doesn't work well, AM radio is pronounced dead—or fit for talk only.

AM radio arose from a tradition of program orientation and a variety of services. After decades of obscurity, FM radio finally caught fire in the late sixties and seventies, accompanying the growth of the home-entertainment system from a hobbyist's toy to a universal home appliance. FM arrived as part of the home stereo system and so was perceived as an adjunct to it—an alternative to listening to tapes or records and used in the same way: to provide a "texture" or background accompaniment to mentally demanding tasks—from the conversation at the family dinner table to an office workday environment. This is as true for rock formats as for soft music formats, and as a consequence, FM programming since the seventies has proved most effective for adults when it's appropriate to these listener expectations and uses.

For FM, then, few interruptions, minimal use of production aids, minimal use of deejays (often limited to liner cards), little or no news coverage outside of morning drive time, minimal contrast from recording to recording, and so forth, typified the approach of most successful stations. I recall when a top-rated FM album rock station tried to update itself in the eighties with some of the then-evolving "modern rock" and met with a wall of listener opposition. The new genre introduced too much contrast and variety into the station's texture and proved a disruptive influence on listeners' use of the station. The modern rock was removed.

Unfortunately, what worked well with FM was usually then tried on AM radio, where it really didn't work well at all. That's because adult listener expectations, as I mentioned, remained and still remain different for AM stations. Listeners switch to AM when involved in such boring tasks as mowing the lawn, washing the dishes, driving to work, and performing repetitive and unsatisfying work. They tune in AM because they are bored and want involving content, interaction, excitement, relevant information, and musical contrast and variety. Even the twenty-five to thirty-four age group has this expectation.

Successful FM techniques work no better on AM than the AM techniques work on FM. However, most radio executives totally misunderstand, assuming wrongly that these failures mean that music programming will no longer work on AM radio, and they retreat to the miscellaneous talk formats and extremely specialized niches that have become the bane of AM.

As it happens, talk formats do contain the elements I've outlined that listeners expect of AM, and so they do work on AM. However, as several spectacular failures have shown, they don't work well on commercial FM stations due to the expectations listeners have of FM stations and the way they use them.

If you are to program an AM station, understand that music programming, even mass-appeal formats such as Adult Contemporary and Country, can still work well on AM—if they are designed to meet listeners' expectations of AM radio. When music formats are done properly on AM, FM may actually find itself at a competitive disadvantage because "being interesting"—an AM programming plus—can actually lose audience on FM.

No more than 20 percent of the audience in any market is interested in talk radio (usually even less). For this reason, only two or three talk stations can survive, let alone prosper, on the AM band in any given locality. However, roughly one-third of all radio listening involves AM radio even today. Thus there is still plenty of opportunity for making a success of a shrewdly programmed music station on AM, despite conventional thinking. (This approach to programming AM has met with success in a number of markets, but many broadcasters have dismissed each success as a fluke. If AM is dying, it's radio people who are killing it.)

For both owners and programmers, the greatest opportunities in radio for the twenty-first century may well be found in today's AM for several reasons:

1. Eighty percent of radio listening is to music. If programmed as explained above with a strong market-saturating AM signal, there is a significant share of audience to be had for music formats on AM.
2. Buying FM stations today tends to be extremely expensive, leading to indebtedness that even profitable operations may not overcome. AM stations, on the other hand, are usu-

ally sold for less than their money-making potential, thus improving the chance of making a profitable business of an AM station.

3. AM stations are unlikely to be left behind in the transition to digital broadcasting, which should disproportionately enhance the eventual value of AM stations in comparison to FM stations. As early as 1993, the USA Digital Consortium successfully demonstrated a very impressive, practical, "in-band, on-channel" system for AM radio over an AM transmitter that simultaneously broadcast conventional AM.

I've tried to make two points in this discussion of FM versus AM programming opportunities. First, as an AM programmer you have a great many more options and opportunity than you may have believed in what's thought of today as an "FM world." Second, if you can truly get inside the heads of your listeners and perceive radio as they do, it's not that difficult to create a successful radio service.

The Importance of Unconventional Strategy

There's a third point involved here, and it's the final programming principle I offer you in this chapter: The greatest opportunity always lies where your peers are not looking for it. In the world of investing, they call this concept "contrarianism." It is based on the proven principle that when the crowd discovers a hot investment, the opportunity in it is just about over.

To put it another way, to succeed, you have to go where the crowd is not because you can't be a leader by being a follower. It may require research and much thought to find a successful idea, and it certainly is not as easy as following the crowd and copying what seems to be working elsewhere. However, by the very fact of your station's being different, it is much easier for you to clearly position it for your listeners with something unconventional—and this always offers more opportunity for success.

Furthermore, by using unconventional strategies to win—methods not fashionable in the radio industry—your success will invariably demoralize your competition ("Hey, that's not supposed to work. Nobody's doing that. Why is it working?"). More often than not, your competitors will react to your success by discarding the very elements of their own programming that made them successful, leaving them unable to compete effectively with you. (Half of winning in radio programming, as in war, is making your opponent lose.) After all, the listener has no idea what is unfashionable in the radio business, and intelligently using ideas not in fashion with other broadcasters will simply strike the listener as fresh and distinctive on both AM and FM bands.

Conspicuous success is what builds a programmer's reputation. What it takes to get there is an understanding of how the listener perceives radio—and especially your station: consistency in execution, and a healthy dose of contrarianism. In the following chapters, we'll explore ways of achieving your programming goals using these principles and the techniques that arise from them. You'll also learn how to bring out the best in your staff, how to be an effective leader, how to "grade" your work with ratings, how to get the rest of the station—including the sales department—on your team, and much more.

Structuring Your Station and Creating Identity

2

The Role of Structure

As mentioned in the previous chapter, the essence of programming is establishing—and then fulfilling—listener expectations. That's what makes audiences tune your station in, listen long, and listen often. The stronger the expectations you arouse—and then meet—the better the result. How can you build clear, concrete expectations of what the station represents in the mind of the listener?

Radio communicates simultaneously at both the rational/conscious and the emotional/subconscious levels—in fact, the same way poetry does. Rational expectations can be built through the use of tools such as descriptive "liners"—simple, repeated statements of what the station offers: "Never more than two commercial breaks per hour." "Where local news comes first." "The one station everyone at the office can agree on." To some extent, your station is what you say it is. However, the far more powerful expectations are the emotional ones. It's futile to try to argue audiences into listening again; they must feel good about listening. It's important for the rational and the emotional elements of a station to be in harmony with and reinforce one another.

For example the most influential programmer of the sixties, Bill Drake, promised "much more music" (rationalized description) and massacred the competition in that decade as his streamlined, music-intensive Top 40 approach (the emotional fulfillment) spread from station to station across the country. The listeners had never been approached that way before by a Top 40 station. Until then, they had usually associated successful Top 40 radio with lots of commercials, so they were easily persuaded that their reason for listening was the music and that "much more music" was what they wanted.

However, just as kids will tell you that what they want for dinner is much more dessert, when listeners do get "much more music," they eventually get bored with it. They want variety, just as kids eventually want something other than dessert all the time.

Thus, although the Drake format swept the country, demolishing the old-line "personality" Top 40s, a lot of damage was left in its wake. When the Drake operations began their ascendancy in the first half of the sixties, the stations they beat had had audience shares in the 20s and 30s. After they surpassed their competitors in the ratings, the victory was generally with smaller audience shares—10s and 15s—and the stations they beat had by then even less audience. In other words, when logically persuaded that what they wanted was "much more music," listeners shifted allegiance. In the end, however, they found the reduction in "personality" and companionship that usually resulted to be boring at the emotional level, and they drifted off to other more specialized formats in hopes of finding "more music" which was more precisely targeted to their own preferences.

What you seek to influence with radio programming is audience behavior, and for that you must provide an emotionally satisfying companionship service—a soundtrack for the listener's life—that logical liners can then reinforce. To begin with, you must consider the structure of the radio station's hour. The structure is the "package" into which the "product"—the radio station—is put, and it is the *package* that defines any product.

To draw a parallel from retailing, if you put the exact same soup in a Campbell's can and in a can labeled "Apex Soup," chances are that consumers will always prefer the soup from the Campbell's can—even if they taste both of them. That's not only because, as Al Reis and Jack Trout point out in *Positioning: The Battle for Your Mind*, "you taste what you expect to taste," but also because the packaging (which includes the brand name and its logo style) arouses very clear expectations of the product based on past experience, which the product in the can will satisfy and reinforce when it is tasted.

The unknown brand name on the other package arouses no positive expectations, other than that it is trying to copy the leader. Tasting that soup will only reinforce that expectation (because it tastes like Campbell's) and will probably lead to the perception that it isn't quite as good because it's a copy. The resulting expectation is that, in the future, the off-brand soup can't possibly taste any better than Campbell's—and probably won't taste as good. Thus the customer will continue to pay more to buy Campbell's.

To make any competitive headway, the Apex Company would have to come up with a tasty soup that is quite different from Campbell's, design a package to epitomize the difference, and then make sure that the positive expectations for their soup are met and satisfied with each experience. Some soup makers have competed successfully against Campbell's, which owns most of the market, by doing this. Pet Milk's Progresso Soups are one example; the Lipton dry ("created fresh") soups are another.

Why should you start designing the station's programming by working on the structure of the hour? In radio, your package is the structure of the station on the air. Station jingles, when used in a particular and consistent way, are very good at creating structure. Bill Drake "jingled into" every record on the successful Top 40 stations discussed earlier—even if his stations were playing several records in a row—thus breaking the hour down into the smallest possible structural pieces. This was a very shrewd strategy, and Drake wasn't the first to do this. Mike Joseph had introduced a similar strategy years earlier at WABC in New York, "jingling out" of every record, and Ron Jacobs had been doing the same thing at the Colgreene stations in the western United States.

Structure is in the details. Where are the spot breaks? How are they handled? What is the station called on the air? (Be consistent.) What wording is used to introduce the newscast, and is there a "sounder," or musical introduction, associated with it? Program directors are notoriously intolerant of air talent taking liberties with planned structural elements like these—and rightly so because these are the key elements that define the station in the mind of the listener. Any distinctive stylistic element that the station uses on the air in a consistent way can help define the station.

For the structural elements that you decide to use, look for things that other stations don't do. Often, the place to look is in the past. Most radio people want to seem up-to-date and "cutting edge" to their peers in the business, but radio listeners don't know what's fashionable in the business and what isn't. When you do something on the air that makes sense to the listener and causes the station to sound distinctive and different, it's to your definite advantage if your competitors perceive it as old-fashioned. This will cause them to underestimate you, and they won't counter your moves, which makes it a lot easier for you to sneak up on them and pass them in the ratings.

Here's an example of what I'm talking about. In the fifties and sixties, one radio fashion for a while was the use of "time signatures" when giving the time—such as, "It's 10:24, WXXX More Music Time." The tag after the time in that phrase is called the "signature," and it actually originated back in the pre-TV days of radio when time checks were sold to advertisers ("10:24, Bulova Watch Time").

In one successful programming venture not long ago, I adapted this old, unfashionable idea for a new station, using it to build structure and enhance community awareness. The way I implemented it, there was always an index card with a time-signature line posted near the digital clock in the control room. The time was always tagged with whatever line was currently posted, such as, "9:31, WXXX Summer Time." The four generic time signatures I used were based on the seasons—spring, summer, autumn, winter—but these were used only when no other, more specific line was posted.

Using resources from the state department of tourism, I developed a list of every civic celebration and planned event in the station's coverage area for the whole year, and I posted a special time signature when each event was in progress ("WXXX County Fair Time"). With many time checks every hour, the station associated its call letters strongly with localities and civic events. If more than one event was going on at the same time, I'd devote one day's time signatures to one event, the next day's to another, and so forth.

Not only did this make the station sound amazingly involved in all civic activities throughout the entire region, but the time signature "salute" became greatly sought after by chambers of commerce and civic groups. It sometimes even got the station an ad schedule or an extra budget for an event that it wouldn't have gotten otherwise. I was the only one who selected the events highlighted, and the time signatures themselves were never sold. That would have cost the station goodwill by diminishing the perceived community commitment.

Time signatures are just one example of how you can use unfashionable programming ideas to succeed. There are other ways. I recall program director Johnny Hyde making use of a "time tone" (a tone or effect which always accompanies the giving of time) at KROY in Sacramento in the early seventies—a concept considered to be hopelessly out-of-date even then. Even odder, the tone was a quick, rising, ripping sound, like somebody knocking a needle off a record. It certainly made the station sound distinctive! Using such offbeat, unfashionable ideas, KROY went on to beat a tough, conventional-sounding competitor that had more power and better coverage.

Back-to-back music segues alone cannot create a structure for a radio station. If your station is the only one in its format in the market, it will perform satisfactorily without much structure—but only until a format competitor enters the market. Unless your station has real audience loyalty, derived from listener expectations that are built and satisfied through structural elements, the tie will always go to the newcomer. If the new station simply does what your station does, with no clearer structure than your station has, listener expectations will simply drop to the level of anticipating what sort of song each station will play next. So subtle changes in the music by the competitor can create stronger music expectations for their station over yours and lure listeners away.

Listeners just don't stay loyal to a music mix. To survive and prosper, your station must have more listener loyalty than is possible by simply how records are mixed together. Your station must project its own personality and establish a clear set of expectations in the mind of the listener, just as Campbell's Soup does in the mind of its consumer. That adds up to hourly structure, or packaging, and consistency in the way that structure is executed.

If structure—the way the station defines its own elements stylistically—still doesn't seem of vital importance to you, think about this: How do you define a glass of water? The product is the water, but, by the phrase itself, you're defining it by the package—the glass. The music, or whatever else forms the core of your station's format, is the product; the distinctive, repeating, anticipatable structural elements of the hour within which it is presented is the package.

The Role of Formatting

The first and most elementary way one radio station is distinguished from another is by its format. What, in very basic terms, does it do? (In listener terms, now; not radio trade terms.)

As noted earlier, modern radio began in the fifties with consistent formats, which easily beat all the well-known block-programmed "variety" stations. Listeners had clearer expectations of what they'd hear when they listened to the format station, and they got what they expected every time they did. All of the structural elements previously discussed in this chapter have to work together harmoniously—artistically—to create in listeners the desired concept of what the station represents, particularly when there's competition in the format.

General managers sometimes suspect that program directors are more concerned with art than commerce, but though the commerce part does pay the bills, the creative elements are what attract and hold an audience. Sticking a sponsored golf report in the middle of a counterculture rock format (I've heard this done!) can destroy the station by contradicting the listeners' established "emotional expectations." There is some art in this. If you lose your listeners while making a quick buck, soon you won't have either listeners or bucks. (There is a connection between the two.)

The Role of Diversity in a Consistent Format

When planning the format structure of your station, please do not read what I have said up to now as indicating that there should be no diversity in what your station offers. In fact, there is some crossover between formats. For example, there are talk elements—such as news—that work in a music format. You should include as many diverse elements as you can, as long as they are consistent with station goals and the lifestyle of your audience.

Make news work for you in a music format. Music listeners like to know what is going on, and they expect radio to be the first medium to tell them about it. Local news is the part that usually interests listeners the most, and the aggressive presentation of local news makes the station seem more involved in the community. That, in turn, helps build listener loyalty and repeat listening in order to keep up with "what's going on." The key is to present the news in a manner that meets the expectations of your listeners. The news thus becomes another structural element through its consistent placement in the hour, consistent style of presentation, and consistently distinctive and reliable content. With news, as well as other content elements, find out what's important to your target listeners, and then include what they want to hear in your format package in an intuitively, emotionally harmonious way.

The Problem with Sports

That brings me to sports play-by-play programming, long a radio staple. I spent seven years working for an organization that believed intensely that sports broadcasts were key to the success of its major-market stations because they served to draw in new audiences. The company paid a lot of money to fund research to prove it—and then buried the report when the results proved the opposite.

As I observed in Chapter 1, play-by-play sports is the one great exception to the way listeners use radio: as a companionable, lifestyle soundtrack to whatever they are doing. Even all-talk stations serve such a role. However, radio listeners still think of sports broadcasts as a program, like a TV program. They will listen to whatever station they must to hear the "program" they want. After it's over, they'll tune back to where they usually listen. Sports events can bring in a large temporary cumulative audience—but at a great cost. Here are some of the problems sports play-by-play can cause.

First, the audience tuning in for play-by-play sees no more relevance to being loyal to the radio station that broadcasts their favorite team than they would to a particular TV channel because it carries the World Series. In both cases, the station is simply a conduit, rather than a companion. A common strategy is to hold elaborate contests based on the game on the morning after the broadcast. However, these contests generally attract just the members of the station's usual audience who stayed tuned to the sports broadcast, rather than bring back to the station the temporary game listeners.

Second, play-by-play broadcasts chase off a number of the station's regular listeners, and they are slow to come back when the game is over. Because they aren't listening, they don't know when the game has ended. The temporary listeners will vanish as soon as the game's done, leaving the station with few if any listeners until the regular audience seeps back over many hours. In most cases, the postgame listener void cancels out the potential ratings boost of all of those temporary game listeners.

These problems create a third. Carrying play-by-play means that you interrupt regular programming—and it's the regular programming that constitutes the station's format! This results in less certainty in audience expectations, which translates to long-term audience erosion if the station has effective competition, and risks a general perception that the "main thing the station does" (and that's what *format* is) is sports!

Play-by-play seems to perform less harmfully within a talk format because the game itself is a form of talk. In general, however, outside of the smallest towns, where carrying the local high school team may be a form of genuine community involvement, the only good reason for carrying play-by-play is revenue. Yet, believe it or not, many major stations today are paying more for the rights to carry a sports event than they can earn from the advertising revenue that the event generates. They incur this loss simply to obtain the presumed listener-growth benefit that the games supposedly offer. This is like paying the salary of your executioner.

If you must do it, probably the least hurtful time to run a sports broadcast is once a week on the weekend because weekend listening patterns tend to differ from those of the weekdays. However, it still makes little sense in the long run to compromise your listeners' expectations even on weekends. Regardless of whether such sports events deliver station profit, the damage to the station's format identity in the mind of the listener—leading eventually to audience erosion—is seldom worth it in the long run.

Perhaps you can now see why all-sports formats seldom perform well—at least outside of New York City, where such things as all-dance-music and continuous sports conversation seem to define particular lifestyles not found elsewhere. Even ESPN, the all-sports TV network, obtains most of its weekly ratings during its weekend game broadcasts.

The problems for the all-sports radio format are twofold: There is a sizable audience for sports play-by-play and special sports events, but as we've discussed, the audience listens to the program and leaves, which results in more sporadic listening patterns than in other formats. In addition, the underlying audience that wants to be accompanied by sports conversation throughout the day tends to be very small in most markets. Of course, a 1 share can make you money in a large market and may justify the use of such a low-performance format. In medium and smaller markets, however, a 1 or 2 share simply represents too small an audience to pay the bills.

Quarterbacking Your Team

So far in this chapter, we've discussed the rationale for distinctive and consistent structuring, or packaging, of a station, including phrases and elements of the construction of the broadcast hour. We've also discussed the need for consistency in the way in which the station does what it has chosen to do. Now, it's time to execute the concept you've chosen in a consistent and well-defined manner. Usually, this calls for what I call a "format book," or programming handbook. This is a manual that not only tells the staff how the structural elements are to be presented, but explains the rationale behind them.

I find that many program directors are afraid to put an explanation for these elements in writing for several different reasons: (1) "If I explain it, the competition may get their hands on it, and they'll counterattack with this information"; (2) "If I try to explain it, the staff may think I don't really know what I'm doing"; (3) "How can I explain it when I've just copied it from some other station somewhere else and don't know why it works?"

If you're afraid of what might happen if the competition should see your handbook, all I can tell you is this: In three decades of programming, during which the manuals I wrote for my various stations must undoubtedly have fallen into enemy hands, never has a competitor ever made competitive use of a format book against me. This is probably because of the "unfashionable" structural elements I invariably used to set my station apart, which led competitors not to take my efforts (or my handbook) seriously until it was too late. My advice is that if you think and program in an original way, it's very unlikely that your competitor will have the wisdom and wit to take competitive advantage of any bootlegged programming information. Any risk of this is far outweighed by the advantages of having your staff understand why they do what you require they do at the station. That understanding not only helps them execute the structure correctly, but results in their feeling like a real team, guided by a plan for success.

If your concern is the second one—fear of staff contempt—then you misunderstand the nature of the relationship between the program director and the airstaff. Your staff will grant you leadership right from the start because you are the designated leader. You don't have to earn leadership; you have it already at the start. What you do have to do is earn respect, and you get that by being open with your airstaff, letting them in on your strategy, and making them feel they are a team following a winning quarterback, even if they feel uneasy about some of your "plays." All they need is to see that you have a clear plan behind those plays.

If your concern is the third one I listed, you are not yet a true program director. If you hope to be one, start analyzing the elements that you're copying from others, and identify the ones that advance your own station-imaging objectives. Then reject those that are only working for the other station because of its market situation or tradition, its competition, or other factors not relevant to your own market. Combine the ones you've decided to make use of with distinctive, compatible elements of your own, and create a station that *others* will copy someday—even though *they* don't understand why it works!

To create your format book, divide it into sections reflecting the major elements of the station's service for which your airstaff has responsibility. Start with a broad statement of the overall format and the station's goals. Then define clearly all of the important format elements, including scripts for the opening and closing of the newscasts and scripts for any other distinctively presented station elements. Weather forecasts can usually be stylized and made more useful to the listener with a customized script. This can better communicate the information provided in those boring communiqués from the weather bureau, which other stations usually read verbatim.

Devote a section of the handbook to your expectations for the airstaff, and don't limit your people to reading liner cards. It may surprise you, but all this careful and exact detail about how key elements of the station's structure must be done can actually free your on-air people to show some real personality: They cannot explore boundaries until they know clearly where the boundaries are. Your air talent cannot improvise effectively in an uncommon situation (an airplane has just crashed near the city; a weather emergency has occurred) until they know what should be kept in and what can temporarily be dispensed with under the circumstances. That comes only with understanding the objectives of the station and its format.

Radio's intimacy can result in a genuine relationship between listener and station that makes the commercials far more effective than is the case with any other medium. Personality is the key to that. A great many people in the radio business think that *personality* means being funny or outrageous. Not at all. It means being relatably "human" for the listener: letting down personal defenses and treating the listener, in on-air comments, like a close friend. Find people with some brains who express themselves interestingly, and put them on the air. That's personality.

When you've finished writing your format book, proofread it for clarity and for spelling (you'll have an easier time commanding respect from your airstaff if it looks as if you know basic English), and then prepare a detailed index to include at the back. Encourage new hires (and existing staff members, as they are introduced to the new procedures) to keep the book with them in the control room for a while so they can consult it when questions arise: "Where do I get the weather forecast? What parts do I use?" "Where do I find the current local news?"

If you want to make sure that your staff executes the station procedures correctly, you must make it as easy as possible for them to do so. In addition, avoid pouncing on them when they fail to follow procedures. When your on-air people make a mistake, try to wait until they're through with their shift to discuss it, and then try to handle the situation in positive terms. Fearful air talent makes for a rotten-sounding radio station—and a lack of teamwork.

If you find someone who doesn't want to be on your team, you must replace him or her with someone who does. To avoid legal problems later, make sure to document for the station's files the conversations, meetings, and behavior that led you to that conclusion. When such a change is clearly needed, it must be made not only for the sake of the station's consistency and atmosphere, but also to maintain the respect of your staff. You must do your best to be human and understanding, but in the end your airstaff must see that you mean what you say and that your rules apply to everyone.

3

Positioning Your Station against the Competition

Hearing Your Station the Way Listeners Do

Unless your station is the only one your audience can receive, you do not program in a vacuum. If there is competition, your job is to differentiate your station—in a positive way—from the others. This does not mean copying the leading station because you just can't beat a leader by copying what it is doing.

As a program director, you have to get a little schizophrenic at this point. Naturally, you cannot compete with a station you haven't listened to, and yet you must not let yourself get obsessed with your competitors. If you do, you'll end up reacting to them, and that's suicide. Your job is to focus on your own station and let the competition react to you.

The starting point, when confronting competition, is to get a realistic concept of how your listeners perceive your station. If you've been at the station for any period of time or if you think only in the radio industry's terms, you'll find this hard to do. I know this from experience. In my first programming assignment in the late sixties, I was program director at my hometown station—the one I'd grown up with and had a lot of affection for. Only by this time, it was getting badly beaten by a newcomer to the market that was copying the then-successful Drake formula for Top 40: a jingle between every record and an airstaff that kept its remarks brief. That station's music wasn't well targeted in my opinion.

Yet, in just a couple of years, it had become dominant, and my station had become an also-ran. Worse, even though my formerly overcommercialized station was now running relatively few spots and the "plays more music" competition had become prosperous and carried a full load of commercials, my research showed that listeners still felt that the competing station played fewer commercials than we did. If you asked the person on the street why they didn't listen to my station, all too often they would respond that it had too many commercials.

That was when I started to learn the lesson that perception is reality. You can't argue people into changing their minds about their perceptions; you can only seek to change their perceptions to match what you believe to be reality. Back then, though, I was still handcuffed by my own perception that my station was clearly the better one in every way. How can you fix a problem that you don't understand?

For me, the solution was to take a day off, get in my car, and drive to a secluded canyon. It was a part of the market I'd never been to before, a complete change of scene. I parked and listened alternately to both stations. The turning point for me came that day. After listening to both stations for hours, I suddenly realized that even though all my station's ingredients were better, they were not as well presented. The other station actually sounded better, and many of the things I hadn't liked about them were, in fact, a part of the reason they were succeeding.

Even now, many years later, I still believe that I was right in thinking that my station was already playing the right hit music for that market and that the other one was not, but there were too many records on my station's playlist, and some weren't played often enough to catch the listener's attention. The biggest hits weren't coming around often enough, and some of the lesser hits were rotating too often.

In addition, there was the matter of station image. The other station's jingle-between-every-record was very repetitive, but it sure created a very strong audience perception of the station's image. (The structure of the hour thus was broken down to the smallest possible unit—just one record—before "repeating.") My station had jingles but no consistent pattern of usage, and about the only really dependable structural elements on my station were the hourly station identification jingles and the news at forty minutes past the hour.

The airstaff on my station was more entertaining and had more ability than the competition, but they lacked a strong station structure within which to work. My personalities were sloppy at times, and they sometimes ad-libbed without having a point. In addition, they tended to have less energy and often displayed little sense of purpose or direction on the air.

Particularly troublesome to me was the incorrect perception of listeners about each station's commercial loads. That demonstrated for me the most important point about programming radio: What people expect of a station is what motivates them to tune in and listen longer and more often, and that's based on their past experience with the station.

Remember the story I told in Chapter 1 about the manager of the self-serve laundry? Here, too, we see that what a station is actually doing at the moment listeners tune in matters very little in meeting or changing perceptions about the station; it's what they expect to happen next that influences their listening behavior. My station, in the listeners' past experience, had run too many commercials (especially for the same few advertisers, repeated too often). The fact that the station now seemed to have few commercials whenever they happened to tune in did not change their expectation that they'd hear plenty of them the next time they tuned in. So, they stayed away.

On the other hand, the competing station "sounded" the same as when they started in the format a couple of years earlier, with jingles before each record (containing the increasingly inaccurate "plays more music" line). Listeners' past experience with the station had been that few commercials were broadcast, and even though the station now often ran at least eighteen minutes of commercials per hour, listeners still expected fewer commercials the *next* time they listened, so they kept tuning back in for "more music."

My challenge in this situation was to build a strong hourly structure for my station to serve as the "package" for my programming "product." I needed to reestablish my station's "brand" and clearly distinguish my station from the other one.

The solution I chose shows a bit about how a station's hourly structure and the way it's executed can change audience perceptions and create fresh expectations, "erasing" the listeners' old experiences with the station. The key, I decided, was to change audience perceptions about the quantity of commercials on each station. That's not because commercials themselves are necessarily objectionable. In fact, I regard it as really dumb to persuade the listener that commercials are undesirable with lines like "WXXX plays fewer commercials" or "KXXX has commercial-free hours." I object to that because once listeners understand that the *station* thinks commercials are bad, they will naturally think negatively about the station whenever it runs a commercial.

Many listeners do not understand why stations run commercials, and some even believe that radio stations are financed by the government. Even those who do understand that the spots are necessary to support the station nonetheless will think of commercials as undesirable when the station uses liners that reinforce that idea, and naturally, they will then react negatively to an advertiser's message every time they hear one on that station. This reduces the effectiveness of the commercials on the station, undercuts the salespeople, and cripples the station as a business. It's a very poor programming strategy.

Actually, I have a surprise for you. If commercials are relevant to the interests and needs of the listeners and to their culture, commercials can be positive elements. In fairness to advertisers and to the station's own image, commercials should be presented as interesting information, which they often are.

So, although I felt that the incorrect listener perception about my station's commercial load was the key to my strategy in this particular programming situation, I did not want to cause negative feelings about commercials themselves. The easy and conventional strategy would have been to use promos and liners to dramatize the lack of commercials on my station, but that would have hurt the station as a sales medium, and so I never considered that.

Consistency Beats Inconsistency

My analysis of the competing station's strength showed that at nights and on Sundays and Mondays, when the station's spot load was low, the station was able to play many records in a row (with jingles between), fully meeting established listener expectations. When they had a full commercial load, however, they "stopped down" after each record (that is, stopped the music or programming) and ran commercials back to back (or double-spotted) each time before jingling back into music. The unpredictability of how many records were played between spot breaks had helped the station maintain its "more music" image, but I saw that this inconsistency could eventually lead listeners to expect commercials between *every* record.

If I succeeded, my station would have to be capable of running a fairly heavy spot load eventually, so I wanted to find a way to project a consistent image of playing a lot of music while accommodating a varying spot load. I was prepared to concede to the competitor their strength—while attacking them at their weak point.

I borrowed my solution from the Beautiful Music stations of the day, and we became the first Top 40 station I know of to adopt fixed "stopdown" points regardless of the spot load. That is, I set the commercial stopdowns at the :10, :20, :30, :40 (within the news), :50, and :00 points of the hour, with a jingle out of each spot break into the music. Rather than claiming "more music"—which not only would have been copying the other guys, but would not have been believed by the audience—I used the indefinite slogan "music power" as the station concept phrase and included it in all of the jingles. This was an affirmative but vague statement about the music on the station, which listeners would have to define for themselves over time.

The format, as I designed it, called for these mandatory fixed spot break positions with at least two records in a row, plus as many more as would fit within the seven or so minutes between each fixed spot break. I instructed the airstaff to stop down for something in these breaks in every hour. If no commercials were scheduled, they were to run a public service announcement (PSA) or a station promo.

My secret weapon in this programming strategy was the consistency of the stop points. Listeners would learn over time that when we played that "music power" jingle, they would always hear at least two records in a row before the next spot break. Listeners would even learn subconsciously where the spot breaks were on my station, and I wanted them to. This unconventional idea was based on the principle that if listeners know when the spots will be run, then they also know when the music will be played. If listeners knew that the spots on my station ran at :10 and :20, for example, then they also knew where the music was in between. That clear understanding led them to stay tuned through the spot breaks, even though each might contain up to four units of commercials or three minutes of spots, whichever was shorter.

The strategy worked. With nothing more than this "different" station structure to distinguish my station from the others, we won back our own community in the ratings in the first year. In the second year, we beat the competition in the two-city combined metro (the competition was licensed to the other city), and in the third year, we beat them in the whole 100-mile-long market by several points—even though the competitor covered all of it, whereas my station was only able to reach 70 percent of the market population.

Every programming situation is different, but the principle needed to win is the same in every competitive situation: Start with the listener's perceptions and expectations of your station and of the competition. Where are competing stations strong and weak? Where are you strong and weak? How can you exploit their weaknesses to your own advantage—without overtly reacting to them?

In the end, both my station and my competitor wound up playing about the same amount of music (though still slightly different songs) and ran about the same number of commercials. However, the two stations sounded different, which meant that each developed its own identity in the listener's mind. If your listeners don't have a clear idea of your station's identity, you'll certainly have a hard time making them loyal and frequent listeners.

Let's review what happened in this example. The strategy was making the other station's weakness—the inconsistency of how many records they'd play between commercials, which varied drastically with the commercial load—my station's strength. Notice that, in return, their strength (they had many breaks because they never had more than two commercials in each spot break) was my weakness (the number of spots on my station would vary in the spot breaks, but the number of spot breaks were the same, in the same places in all hours, and we never omitted spot breaks when we had no commercials to run).

That, in theory, meant that the two stations statistically were equal. The reason we beat them in what should have been a standoff was that our format structure seemed not only clearly different from theirs but also newer than theirs. Novelty gave us the edge. As often happens in situations like this, when a programmer wins with an unconventional strategy, the competition completed our victory by reacting to us—in part, by demolishing the strong image and hourly structure they'd established, by cutting back drastically on their jingle use, and by trashing their hit music image by adding a number of non-hit album rock tracks. Half of winning is making the other guy lose, as I mentioned earlier, and this is fairly easy in radio when you win with something that is "out of fashion" in the industry.

You'll always find your success by starting with, and then molding, the audience's perceptions and expectations of your station and your competition. However, you can only do it through freshness and relentless consistency of presentational style, not through name-calling or the use of logic. Never argue with your listeners.

Radio is a medium "consumed" subconsciously and emotionally; the listener's literal, logical mind is somewhere else while he or she listens. With the conscious mind occupied, radio is soaked up "subconsciously" and almost subliminally. As a soundtrack to the listener's life, radio is perceived through its pattern of presentation, which is where the station's packaging, its hourly structure, comes in. Make that pattern clear, positive, distinctive, and well defined, and you're usually ahead of your competition right from the start.

The Role of Research

Now, let's spend some time on how you can identify the listener perceptions of your station and the competition. The key is audience research. Audience research can take many forms. It can be cheap or very expensive, invaluable or actually misleading. The guidelines given in this section will help ensure that it works properly for you.

Research, to be effective, has to be objective, not biased toward any particular point of view or expected outcome. It has to tell you what the consumers—the listeners—think, not just what the researcher thinks they think. In my experience, professional researchers have problems with interpretation. They rely on logic to explain their findings, even when logic has little to do with listener behavior.

Had a professional researcher been involved in helping devise a strategy for the station in my case study, he or she would have found that most of the potential audience thought that my station had too many commercials. The researcher would probably have recommended that the station cut back on the number of commercials played. However, the station was only playing four minutes of commercials an hour and was going broke, and we probably would have chucked the costly research report into the wastebasket in disgust.

That reaction would have been a mistake because the basic data were correct: Listeners did believe that our station had too many commercials. The fact that their perception varied so greatly from reality actually highlighted the real opportunity for us. When dealing with professional researchers, then, I suggest that you examine the data yourself and reconcile the findings into a pattern of listener perception. Take the professional researcher's "logical" interpretation of the data with many grains of salt.

Research doesn't have to be expensive, and it doesn't even have to be done by a professional researcher. It can be informal like the research in the case study presented earlier. It consisted of lots of (frustrating) listener conversations, followed up by good, hard, really objective listening to both my station and my competitor's, putting aside for a while my own professional beliefs and prejudices.

Designing Your Own Study

Whether you decide to do your own research or elect to hire a firm (or a university marketing department) to do formal research for you, the three parts of the project are the same: (1) defining the goals and designing the questions, (2) obtaining objective information through some sort of interview process or behavior study, and (3) interpreting the results. Let's address each of these parts in turn.

You'll never get any useful research if you haven't a clue what you want to find out! Start there. The goal of the research project is to answer specific questions about your station and others. What are those questions? Boil them down to the smallest possible number; a tediously long questionnaire will result in degraded results, as those who agreed to cooperate get tired of the time and effort it's taking to participate.

If you aren't sure how to focus your questions, have informal and unscientific conversations with listeners before starting to make the questionnaire. Try to spot recurring thoughts and perceptions about your station and others. (In a more formal setting, focus groups can perform this function.)

Once you've figured out what you want to learn more about, design the questions carefully. Keep in mind that what you want to investigate is listener behavior, not listener opinion. When you ask people to report or explain their own behavior, you are asking them to intellectualize something inherently emotional. They may do their best to be honest with you in their answers, but all too often you'll wind up with what they *think,* rather than what they do.

For example, when you ask people what they like to watch on television, they report liking documentaries and quality drama. However, when you hook up a device to their TV set to record their actual viewing habits, you often find them watching lightweight comedies and undemanding game shows. The usual conclusion has been that people lie to researchers to elevate their status. Perhaps some do, but based on my own experiences in research, I find that most people really do try to tell you what they think is the truth.

If so, then, why does this disparity occur? When you ask viewers to think about their favorite TV shows, the ones they remember best are those exceptional programs they are reporting. However, when they come home at night, worn out from working, the last thing they want is to be challenged and enlightened. They're exhausted, and they seek "mind candy" to help them relax, so they watch unchallenging and unenlightening shows. Behavior doesn't match opinion, and the poor folks who choose a situation comedy over a documentary at the end of a busy day probably wouldn't see their preference as an inconsistency. After all, we asked them about what shows they liked best, not the ones they would pick when they didn't want to think after a hard day.

Incidentally, this phenomenon creates a real problem in the most common form of music research: playing fragments, or "hooks," of songs for people over a phone line or—worse yet—in an auditorium. In these situations, the participant has to recognize each song hook, try to recall the whole recording it comes from, and then figure out what he or she thinks of it. After some thought, the listener honestly reports an opinion, instead of behavior. Worse yet, when tested in an auditorium setting, each participant can be influenced by a neighbor's body language or murmured comments.

In fact, I've found that one sign of "intellectualized"—and thus flawed—music test findings done on audiences over the age of twenty-five is the reporting of burnout: the active rejection of overly familiar songs. When they listen to the radio, I find that the mainstream adult listener is not likely to tune away from any song they know and like just because they hear it a lot. Song burnout, as a programming tool, seems to be pretty much a fiction created by intellectualized responses.

To repeat, when designing the questions in an audience research project, always focus on listener behavior rather than opinions. That said, it is not a bad idea to add a few opinion-eliciting questions on the key points you're exploring. Opinions can be useful in interpreting behavior, even though they don't necessarily correlate to actual behavior at all. Use opinion research to cross-check with the behavioral responses and to help you find revealing inconsistencies and paradoxes, such as the "too many commercials" opinion in my case study.

A behavior-oriented question might be, "What radio station do you most often turn to in the morning?" A corresponding opinion-eliciting question might be, "Which radio station do you think has the best morning show in the area?" Another behavioral question: "When you switch away from that station, what sort of thing are you looking for, and on what stations do you usually find it?" An opinion-oriented question: "What do you think of radio station KXXX? What do you think of WXXX?"

When you see a disparity between listener perception and reality, analyze it for its implications. Similar research for a station in Los Angeles once allowed me to discover that although the staff thought they worked for a music station, the music was so irrelevant to its listeners that the audience thought of the station as a talk station. The music was perceived simply as filler. This led to the programming conclusion that the music could be redirected toward the younger audience the station wanted to get without losing a single one of its current older listeners, and that's the way it turned out.

Once you have defined the goals of your research and have designed the questions, the actual study takes place. Generally, if it's an interview-based study, it's done from a script to make sure that the wording stays the same. The wording and question sequence will have an effect on the answers obtained, so they must remain constant throughout the survey for consistent results.

Most people outside radio have a hard time reading a script believably as if it were spontaneous. For that reason, some stations prefer to avoid expensive research companies and do their own perceptual research—not so much to save money as to get the best compliance and quality control. Refusal rates for telephone studies have been increasing steadily in recent years because of the amount of telemarketing being done, and an interviewer who is obviously reading a script will get more refusals than an interviewer who sounds like a courteous and interested human being. The more refusals, the greater the error factor as you get farther and farther from a truly random sample. This sort of probability study demands a randomly selected cross section of the population for statistical accuracy.

The telephone is the most convenient way to conduct interviews, but you'll get a lot of refusals. In addition, people who don't have phones will of course be excluded from the study, skewing the results somewhat. That's because those who don't have phones tend to differ in various ways from those who do, and that could include tastes in radio and music. However, all of the major radio rating services now in business fail to reach those nonphone homes too, and the advantages of telephone-based surveying usually outweigh the disadvantages.

One disadvantage that can be overcome concerns unlisted phone homes. Studies indicate that people who have intentionally unlisted phone numbers differ in various psychological ways from those with listed numbers, and the radio survey companies do try to include these unlisted homes in their universe of surveying. This group should be included in your survey, too. The easiest way to do this is the method that the now-defunct Birch survey once used, and that today's successful "second rating service," Willhight Research of Seattle, Washington, still uses: Begin with a random selection of listed numbers for your starting sample, but don't call any of those numbers! Here's what you do. Using the phone book, select the phone number on each page that is a predetermined number of lines below the top of the page in a particular column on the page. Then, change the last numeral downward by a fixed number. For example, change 555-1234 to 555-1232, and change 555-3341 to 555-3339.

By making this systematic adjustment, you eliminate the bias toward listed numbers that your original sample created. Of course, you'll also reach disconnected numbers this way, which is the price you pay for randomization. Radio rating companies eliminate from their surveying all businesses and "group quarters" (dorms and barracks). Due to the unfavorable telephone interview climate of these busy locations, you may want to skip them, too, if and when you reach them.

In-person surveying is more work than using the phone, but it generally yields fewer refusals and greater cooperation. To really do it right, you'd want to adopt an approach similar to the one once used by the Pulse rating service: in-home interviews. This type of interview avoids the biases that arise from interviewing at specific lifestyle locations, such as commercial malls. The technique involves interviewing on residential blocks selected from addresses drawn at random from the phone directory. All of the homes on the block are included except the one in the phone listing you selected. This one step eliminates both the unlisted-home and non-phone-home biases.

With a good interviewer (Pulse drew from the same pool of people as the Census Bureau does), the refusal rate from potential interview subjects should be less than 5 percent. It's no surprise that, using this method, Pulse produced the most accurate radio ratings of any survey company ever. It was expensive to do, though, and the lack of radio station support led to the company's demise in the late seventies. However, this can be a relatively inexpensive technique if you use your own staff or students from a nearby college statistics or marketing class to do the interviewing.

One other form of listener research should be mentioned: focus groups. Focus groups should be used only as "thought starters"—to identify possible listener mind-sets for subsequent research. Not only is a focus group far too small to have any statistical validity, but it's not random either. Those impaneled on focus groups are usually drawn from lists of people who want to participate in such groups—not only to earn money, but to express their opinions.

The greatest hazard of a focus group is the risk that a station executive sitting behind the one-way glass will hear an opinion expressed by the group that matches his or her own, will see this as confirmation of that opinion, and will immediately make a bad decision about the station as a result. That's just human nature. It happens often—and not just with general managers either. It can happen to you! Treat anything you hear from a standard five- to fifteen-person focus group with a lot of skepticism until you are able to verify it with reliable research.

That is not to say that you must do research in the conventional manner. As you have figured out by now, I propose that the best program directors look for unconventional ways to reach their goals, and that includes audience research. The best way to approach any radio problem—and probably any problem you'll ever encounter—is to identify your goal first and then work backward to find a workable, reliable method to reach it.

For example, I have had great success in music research using a "reverse focus group" method that I've trademarked as ReFocus™. This approach does away with the need to maintain statistical validity, yet still allows reliable and accurate results to be generated inexpensively from a small group. The key in this case is impaneling only people who are "prequalified"—that is, firmly established, using definite criteria, as being right at the core of the audience target—and then using an interview setting that's casual and doesn't cause the group to start intellectualizing their emotional, behavioral responses. The researcher must ensure that the participants treat the occasion as an informal, social gathering in which conversation occurs, rather than as a serious and important event in which they are interviewed. Naturally, you'll have to find your own way to prequalify your subjects if you use an approach like this, and you'll also have to develop a way of cross-checking them to make sure that the group stays "on target" and doesn't start intellectualizing their own behavior.

Perhaps you'll find a completely different, unconventional way of doing research that yields results that you find reliable. If you do, use it.

If you choose to have audience "perceptual research" done by a professional research firm or a college statistical class, remember to place most of your confidence in the gathering and tabulation of the raw data. Be skeptical about any accompanying "interpretation and recommendations" you receive from the researcher. Like many salespeople and general managers, professional interviewers are very logical and rational. They do a fine job setting up the study and tabulating the results, but they often totally miss inferences, paradoxes, and implications in the data. They'll usually give literal and logical interpretations that can lead you to absolutely the wrong course of action.

Radio is "consumed" by the listener with the right brain—the inaccurately named "unconscious mind"—and behavior and emotional response (right brain functions) are what we, as program directors, are trying to understand. The "right brain" of our listeners is what we are learning to communicate with, using every element of programming employed at our station.

In this chapter, we've looked at packaging a radio station, and the key principles in developing a strategy to create a clear identity for the station and to position it versus its competition. We have also considered how to determine what's in the audience's minds already about our station and its competition. You can't get anywhere by directly and rationally contradicting what the listener thinks, but you can repackage the station to emphasize its strong points and freshen it with respect to the other stations, thus altering listener perceptions. The starting point is existing listener perceptions.

Whatever strategy you come up with will probably be executed by an airstaff. Of course, it is possible to automate a station in a very sophisticated way using a desktop computer, but then you may lose one or both of the greatest strengths of a station: the one-to-one human contact between an on-air personality and a listener, and the local flavor of the station. In the next chapter, we'll assume that you're going to be the captain of a team, and not of a computer. How will you lead your team?

4

Leading an Airstaff

Working with Creative People

Some program directors actually prefer automation because it means that they always have a completely obedient "airstaff." In fact, many radio stations are virtually one-person operations. Other program directors prefer to hire "liner card readers" of limited talent because they are very compliant and easy to work with.

It is harder to deal with talented people. They tend to have intelligence and minds of their own. However, these are the people who have personality; these are the interesting people who can translate listening to your station into a personal, involving experience for the audience. Are you afraid to hire someone whom you perceive as having more talent than you do? Surprise! That's exactly the person you should hire for on-air work. You should assemble the strongest on-air team you can. Your own talent should be in coaching and directing that team.

If you are the strongest personality on the air, you've made a serious mistake in putting your airstaff together. This mistake is usually made by program directors (PDs) who are unsure of their own ability to lead others and who seek to guarantee their authority by being the clear "star" of the airstaff. These PDs tend to be extroverted. They often enjoy social events, and they generally enjoy having people look up to them.

Incidentally, this is a fairly common mistake that sales managers make, too. Some individuals in this position repeatedly hire people who just never seem to sell well, with the result that the sales manager is always the top biller on the station. When that happens, the station never makes as much money as it should. As with a good PD, a good sales manager should be a coach. He or she should not be competing with the sales staff, but instead should be developing them.

Competition between the PD and the airstaff is not the only problem that this type of PD has; even worse, he or she has a really hard time hearing the station the way the person on the street does. PDs of this type believe that their job is either to copy programming ideas that seem to be working somewhere else or to "individualize" their station by tailoring it to their own taste, leaving the listener out of the equation. If you recognize yourself in this description, I urge you to spend a lot of time talking to listeners of your own station and those of other stations—in places other than your usual haunts—to start getting perspective on how people outside your own circle perceive your station.

For the PD of the opposite psychological mind-set—a PD who is somewhat introverted—the most common mistake is somewhat different: a tendency toward "leadership through fear." PDs of this type lack confidence that the staff respects them, and so they act distant and arbitrary. There may be a red phone in the control room, and the PD uses it to keep the staff in line. This programmer doesn't seem to realize that the only way to get respect is to earn it, and that by demanding respect, you lose it.

Every team *wants* a leader and will give him or her the benefit of the doubt, at least at the start. You should neither seek to be a close friend of the people you lead, nor should you be unfeeling toward them. As in any endeavor, the coach is something of a parent figure and leads by example.

Following Your Own Rules

This brings us to the one mistake that both of these otherwise opposite types of program directors often make: They permit themselves to do things on the air that they forbid their staff to do. Their excuses include, "Well, I do the morning show" and "I have more talent/judgment/experience than my staff, so I know how to do it" and even "It's my rule, so I can break it." Whatever the rationalization, refusing to follow your own rules is a sure way to lose the respect of your staff.

You make the rules for the airstaff; you must follow your own rules when you are on the air. It's as simple as that. Your staff will look to you to set an example for them and to demonstrate how it should be done. Don't fail them.

Using the Format Book

Let's discuss two additional points. In Chapter 2, I mentioned the format book—the handbook that explains how the programming is to be executed and why. I mentioned that many PDs object to such detail because they fear that their secrets will wind up in their competitors' hands, and I told you why this should not be a major concern for you. The other, much less discussed reason why PDs don't write such books is that they haven't thought through the programming detail themselves! They throw new hires into the control room and assume that they'll pick up enough from other staff members to "do it right" on the air. This practice results in a sloppy, inconsistent station and an airstaff that is frustrated because they can never seem to please the boss.

If you haven't taken the time to think through, in great detail, how you want the station to sound and why, then you truly cannot expect the airstaff to figure it out for themselves to your satisfaction. At best, everyone will come up with a different version. Think it through, write it down, add an index, and pass it out to your staff. It's the game plan! Note the questions that come back to you about it; the ones that recur tell you where you need to be clearer. Revise the format book until you get the result you want on the air. Some PDs distribute the format book in a loose-leaf binder so that pages can easily be added or changed.

Setting the Mood

The other point I want to discuss is my observation that the mood that your airstaff projects is the mood that the listeners feel. That's the transactional analysis principle I mentioned in the Preface—and possibly radio's greatest strength: People respond to you as you present yourself to them. It's true in person, and it's even more true on the radio, where listeners cannot see the person talking to them and thus do not receive mixed messages through clothing, appearance, and body language.

All that listeners can relate to on the radio is the voice, and that can be consciously controlled. Thus, the rapport that talented on-air people can build between themselves and listeners can be very strong. Of course, this rapport should be wrapped in attitudes that listeners enjoy feeling; this requires confident air talent who feel securely part of a motivated team. You control the attitude of your staff in the same way that a good sports coach molds the attitudes of a sports team. The team picks up and reflects your attitude. Present yourself accordingly.

You know that red phone in the control room? Don't use it. Try to avoid calling your staff while on the air. There are a few obvious exceptions. If an on-air person is doing something illegal, is doing something that can cause immediate problems for the station, or is making a significant error over and over again (mispronouncing an important local name, for example), you'll have to call and fix it. Even then, try to keep the mood light, and say something complimentary or at least pleasant before addressing the problem. People on the air are performing before an audience they can only imagine; their mood can easily be crushed (and the mood they project is the mood the listener feels). Keep their mood upbeat and pleasant—not angry or fearful or nervous or ashamed.

There is a downside to empathizing with your airstaff, which of course is something you should be doing, and that is the impulse to put their needs and wants above those of the station. Remember that you are not only the coach of a team, but also the paid representative of the ownership and management of the station. Seek the win-win scenario. Don't play scrooge with your airstaff, but don't give away the store to them either.

Pay and Unionization

In my experience, what the staff seeks most from their coach is understanding and support. Thoughtfulness and pride in the team can count for more than a raise, believe it or not. When there isn't the money available for the salaries you'd like to pay or the equipment you feel you need, I believe you'll be better off by being frank with the airstaff about the station's economic situation. There's a good chance that they don't see the business side of the station. They may believe that there is a pot of money somewhere to provide salaries and any benefits the owner feels like handing down and that the owner's greed is responsible for anything less than they see as reasonable.

Most stations seem to want to keep the profit picture from their on-air people. If the station is losing money, management may worry that staff members will fear it is failing and will bail out; if the station is making money, management may fear that the staff will want more money than they are getting. However, if it is possible to inform the staff about the economic goals of the station and the current situation (even if only generally), my experience is that the airstaff will be quite capable of understanding it and will try to help meet the goal as much as their assignments permit.

I also believe, based on my experience, that when the airstaff sees the station gaining in prosperity and when the station has been frank and honest with them, they will perceive a link to their own prosperity. Why not work with your general manager to develop a profit-sharing plan through which a certain percentage of any after-tax profit is divided among the staff (all staff, not just airstaff)? This is a more productive approach than the traditional year-end bonus, which is usually not linked to achievement in any way discernible to the staff, and it need not amount to more than such a bonus would be.

A word about unionization. Generally, it's the large-market stations that become unionized, although I have seen some pretty intense organizing activities at smaller stations when the staff feels ill-treated and seeks representation. The reason why it's usually the larger stations that the unions target is that the dues they receive tends to be a significant amount only at big operations. I'm bringing up the matter of unionization because there are some really negative things associated with union shops in radio.

Station managers usually do not welcome unionization. When a labor union acts as intermediary between the airstaff and the station on economic issues, the collective bargaining process often creates an adversarial relationship between the two parties. The station managers are often seen as miserly and uncaring, and the airstaff responds by demanding money and other benefits that the station may not be able to afford. On-air people with this attitude may not relate to listeners as well as they might, which could affect the attitude of station's audience and the station's effectiveness as an advertising medium.

I've often found that broadcast unions appear to believe it to be in their own interest to promote and maintain this type of adversarial relationship—not only as a bargaining tool, but as a means of retaining the perceived need of union representation. Therefore, although few union people will admit it, there is generally no incentive for the union to help build morale and company pride at the station—and these are essential ingredients for a winning station—because a happy and charged-up staff could make the union seem unnecessary.

Here, then, is some specific advice concerning unionized stations. If your station already has a union, avoid being critical of it. It's a fact of life. If you appear to be anything less than fully accepting of the situation, you will only aggravate the perceived adversarial relationship. Try to give your airstaff a little bit more than the union requires, in treatment as well as money, to make it subtly clear through deeds rather than words that staff members do not owe everything they have to the demands of the union.

However, be sure to read the contract. Be aware that certain types of voluntary preferential treatment can become contractual. For example, if the airstaff is paid for forty hours a week, but you develop the habit of only assigning thirty-seven hours a week—or if you chronically let the staff go home before the appointed hour—labor law often holds that the salary the airstaff receives is paid for the hours customarily worked. If you then begin to enforce a forty-hour week, you may have to pay overtime for the difference. This certainly does not seem fair, but this is usually the decision in such situations if an employee files a grievance on the matter. Be a generous boss, but avoid setting precedents that can turn your attempt to be generous into a grievance that the union wins and the station loses.

If your station is not unionized, handle your staff in such a way that they are unlikely ever to seek redress by bringing in a union. The station will always be better off if the staff perceives it as being as generous as possible and an enterprise in which they have a stake and to which they are loyal.

The key issue that sparks unionization talk at stations is pay. I've already suggested that you put your airstaff in the "economic loop" of the station as much as possible: Not only should they have a realistic idea of how fairly the station is paying them, but they should also understand that they will be rewarded as the station increases its profits. In addition, staff members must believe that you are fair and evenhanded on pay issues with new hires and evening air talents as well as your drive-time and daytime people.

There is a tradition in radio that the morning air talent gets the best pay. I would feel comfortable with such a pay differential only if everyone on the airstaff agreed that this was a fair situation, which seldom happens. I've tended to go in the opposite direction and establish a single starting pay level for all airstaff, with a raise structure announced up front, based on tenure at the station, so that the longer a person stays, the more he or she makes. This benefits the station by adding stability to the airstaff and provides an incentive for the staff to stay.

The profit-sharing ideas suggested earlier would be over and above salary, based on how the station has done during the year. In contrast, the raise structure would be fixed and understood by all, just like other benefits that the staff routinely receives.

In many cases, the morning personality is the key for the purposes of the station's ratings and economic success. I've found that just holding this prestigious position can be its own reward. I always hire on-air people who could work any shift. I start new hires on the least prestigious shift—all-nights or evenings—promoting them to middays, afternoons, and mornings as those ahead of them leave. I refuse to have a pay scale that tells some on-air people that they are less important than others.

If you're with the majority in this business, you don't agree. If you plan differential pay scales based on the perceived value of each shift, then for heaven's sake be consistent on what the pay differential is. Give current staff every opportunity to apply for the better-paid airshifts as they become available, so that your people perceive the pay differential to represent the prestige and value of the time period and not themselves as individuals. The differential then provides an incentive to stay with the station and strive for promotions to better-paying positions. You can't build a team if everybody resents everybody else. This leads to cliques and destructive personnel situations.

The second most common reason for an airstaff to seek union representation is the overall treatment by the station, especially in terms of scheduling. Again, if the staff understands your effort to be fair, this should not be a problem. Fairness includes scheduling yourself for work when needed rather than overloading the staff with extra work so you can have a day off.

A common airstaff scheduling procedure in radio is the six-day week. Employees are assigned to work six and a half hours a day, six days a week, to ensure that some full-time airstaff work on the weekend and to reduce the expenditure and reliance on part-timers. A union would generally demand five work days per week as the only acceptable full-time approach, which would require overtime pay for a sixth day. Many nonunion stations have chosen to give the sixth day off on a fixed pattern—every second, third, or fourth weekend day off—in response to the airstaff's desire to have a full weekend off. Be aware that if you do this and then need to omit the regular weekend day off occasionally because of vacations or illness, labor law might require overtime pay for that "normal day off" if it is worked after all, even if the individual works fewer than forty hours per week.

The On-Air Program Director

If you are like most PDs, you are one of your own part-timers— plugging the holes and filling the gaps when nobody else can work. If you are diligent and work the part-time shifts until you find a part-timer who meets your standards, I salute you. You'll probably go far in this business. Many PDs will hire inadequate people if necessary, to avoid working the extra hours themselves, even if the station sounds bad as a result.

If you're like most PDs in American radio, you also have a regular airshift of your own. Relatively few stations outside the biggest markets can afford the luxury of having an off-air PD anymore. Those that do sometimes change their minds and decide that an off-air PD can be replaced by one of the airstaff as a cost-saving measure. It may actually help your longevity as a PD if you are also one of the air talents; then you will seem less expendable.

In any on-air work that you do, you must follow your own rules for air personalities. Don't bend them even a little bit. You are setting an example for your staff—and communicating the importance of the rules you lay down—every time you're on the air.

I do understand that it is very difficult for an on-air PD to do a really good, creative on-air show because this requires not only significant time to prepare for the show, but also your undivided attention while it is in progress—and everybody wants to talk with or see the PD while you're on the air. Although you should have a firm policy of not allowing any airstaff to be interrupted during a show at any time—a policy that should have the general manager's endorsement and that should be enforced—the PD is usually seen as the exception to the rule because of the other administrative responsibilities of the job.

You will face many distractions from the general manager, the salespeople, your own airstaff, and important phone calls that you may need to take while doing a show. Your strict attention to following your own rules will be your "saving grace" in executing a presentable show while you are being distracted.

Who Critiques *Your* On-Air Work?

You cannot fully command the respect of your airstaff if you don't work at keeping your own on-air work at the highest level. Who critiques the program director? First and foremost, you do. Make airchecks regularly, and listen to them. Spot your own laxities, and fix them. Identify areas in which you need improvement, and work on them. In addition, your boss should critique your on-air work. Ask your general manager for comments and input from time to time, and take them for what they seem to be worth. (If the general manager is qualified to judge on-air work, this can help you a lot.) Finally, if your station has a consultant, he or she should critique you. If not, your peers in the business who are expert at critiquing can do it—if you're confident that they'll be honest enough to give it to you straight.

Bear in mind that each PD, consultant, and general manager has his or her own interpretation of what's good and bad on the air, and someone may criticize something you do on the air that you believe to be correct and right. Use your own judgment, but be open to informed criticism.

Critiquing Your Staff

Listen with an open mind, but with the same reservations, to the feedback you hear about your airstaff's work. Something you may have gotten used to in someone's on-air work may represent sloppiness, laziness, or inattentiveness in their work, and you may need an outside comment to become aware of it. Consultants, if good at what they do, have great value in offering a fresh and unbiased perspective. However, they are usually not in a position to take into account local factors and longevity considerations in any unusual aspects of a station's operation—factors that may be working for the station's success, even though they might not work in other places or under other circumstances.

Of course, the primary source of direction and development for all air talent on your station remains you, the program director. I know a number of PDs who seldom offer any input of any sort to part-timers or to those who work the fringe shifts, such as evenings or all-nights.

Your staff does need your input! If everything is fine, don't forget to tell them so. If there are problems from time to time, critiques and suggestions then have the proper, positive context. If all your staff hears from you are criticisms, they will presume that you don't like them or that they cannot please you, and they'll start looking for another job. More than one PD has said to me over the years, "If I say nothing to them, they should know that I like what they're doing." In fact, they won't. Would you, if the situation were reversed?

Choosing a New On-Air Person

Directing your staff starts with selecting them. Of course, when you accept a job as a program director, the on-air people are generally already in place. You may have to work with them to develop them as you want them. Be sure to give them ample time to meet your expectations before deciding that you must make a change.

To me, the first step in developing air talent is hiring them. If you hire people who prove to be inadequate, it's your own fault unless they actually misrepresented themselves to you. As a PD, I regard it as my own personal failing if I find I have to fire somebody I hired because they can't do the job. I deeply regret having to penalize an employee for a mistake I made in choosing them.

Therefore, carefully consider every potential hire. If you aren't sure that they have what you need, ask for another tape. If you can afford to, bring the applicant to the station for an interview, but in any event, do an in-depth interview on the phone. You need to know the applicant as a person as well as a potential employee (team member) in order to make a good decision.

Reviewing the Applicant's Submissions

New PDs sometimes wonder how they can use a telescoped aircheck tape, running perhaps only three to four minutes, to make a good hiring decision. Here are a few thoughts about what to listen for. First, the tape submitted with an application should be typical work. What you want to hear—and what experienced on-air people know you want to hear—is what they would sound like on your station if you tuned in at random and they didn't know you were listening. The tape should represent typical work, not best work. That establishes a level of competence. Beginners have a tendency to make a "Whitman Sampler" tape—one great record intro, one great spot, one great joke, and so on. Not only does this sort of tape assembly give away a beginner, but because it was made by striving for a level of performance the applicant seldom attains, the execution often sounds uneven, off-balance, or awkward.

With a mandatory aircheck tape, the applicant must submit a résumé. A résumé of more than one page is usually an indicator of lack of experience. I've found that the length of the résumé usually varies inversely with the amount of the applicant's experience! A résumé should always be limited to no more than one page. Read the résumé for "puffery." If there seems to be a lot of description about what a past job entailed, particularly if it is material insignificant to *your* opening, that also suggests a lack of experience. A padded resume is a danger sign. This person does not feel qualified for your job and wants to appear as something he or she is not. Such a person most likely will try to *be* someone they are not while on the air, which will really alienate your listeners.

But first, listen critically and carefully to the audition tape submitted. A good audition tape by a deejay should include an aircheck and some production. Because recording commercials is generally an important part of the job, the applicant should show that he or she knows how to do it. If there is no production, request some samples before making a decision. If reading news is an important part of the job, ask for a news aircheck too. A surprising number of otherwise competent and even talented deejays are intimidated by the need to read news—as if this were different from reading commercials or anything else on the air. If the applicant can't read news without lots of stumbles, this will affect your decision.

Something that used to be mandatory in an aircheck was the assurance that the breaks are consecutive. Because the records and irrelevant spots are "telescoped"—with only the starts and finishes of each on the tape edited together for speed in listening—you may want to make sure that a seemingly satisfactory aircheck wasn't assembled from among many different "takes" or shows. Today, however, so many stations run "cold segues" (two or more records played back-to-back with no interruption) that you are likely to get many tapes in which the air talent goes into one record and comes out of another one, making doctored tapes harder to spot.

If the tape appears to be doctored, it tells you (1) that this applicant lacks self-confidence and doesn't feel that he or she can do good professional work consistently and (2) that he or she may be right about that. If new hires can't do on your station what they did on their tapes, you are fully justified in firing them on the spot for this minor fraud. However, you're better off spotting the doctored tapes when you hear them and not hiring these folks in the first place.

Creating Your Own Aircheck Tape

By the way, when you need an aircheck tape of yourself, start with a long tape. Begin the dub of the aircheck you'll present at the point where you hit your stride. Even the most professional air talent tends to be a little off-balance knowing that an important aircheck has started, and it takes some time to forget it and get back to normal on-air work.

The policy I recommend is to routinely aircheck every show, start to finish. Insert the cassette in the "skimmer machine" at the start of the shift, and keep it in there until you're through with each show—

turning the tape over each time it reaches the end. Not only do you always have a current cassette of your everyday, routine on-air work whenever you might need it, but if you find yourself suddenly *out of work*, you always have a current tape you can use for an application! (As suggested earlier, be sure to review your own airchecks regularly, to make sure that you're not slipping into bad habits.)

I am assuming that you have a "skimmer machine." For your own benefit and that of your airstaff (and your critiques of their work), you should have one of these in the studio. This is a cassette recorder that only records when the mike is on, thus automatically "telescoping" the tape for you. Many smaller stations don't have one, yet it's cheap and simple to set one up. For this you need only a decent standard-size (not miniature) portable cassette machine; you can usually find a suitable one for thirty to forty dollars at any electronics-supply store. Make sure it's AC-powered so you don't have to rely on batteries for its operation.

To turn it into a skimmer, you'll need a line-level audio input, fitted with a standard miniature phone plug to insert into the "line" or "aux" input (never a microphone input), and a second line, fitted with a subminiature phone plug, which fits into the smaller jack next to the microphone jack. Either shorting or opening the connection between the two wires connected to the subminiature plug will allow the recorder motor to run. Have your engineer wire this cable appropriately to the spare contacts on the control board microphone switch.

When a cassette is loaded into this recorder and set to record, the tape will run when the mike is switched on and will stop when the mike is turned off. The total investment should be under sixty dollars for all parts, including the cassette recorder. Every station should be able to come up with that kind of money for such an essential programming tool.

One more bit of advice concerning the aircheck part of any application that you may send out: Never submit your master tape! Always use a copy of it for applications. Few stations return these tapes. (I have always considered it part of radio etiquette to return aircheck tapes, especially when I advertised for applications in the first place, but this is not common and should never be relied on.) If you send your master tape and the station doesn't return it, your chances of getting a decent job have just disappeared. Not only can't you get in the door of most stations without an aircheck, but the fact that you don't have one because you sent a station your master, even if they promised to return it, labels you as naive and inexperienced.

Checking References

If an applicant has sent you a very acceptable aircheck tape and you are leaning toward hiring him or her, don't fail to check the references. You'd be amazed how seldom PDs do that—and how often that would have made a difference.

I recall a situation not long ago when I received a really impressive aircheck from an air talent at a very small rural station. I almost didn't check his references because I could hear his obvious talent, but I did, thank goodness. The applicant's reference confirmed that he was a terrific talent and said that "it was a shame he had to leave." I asked why he had to leave and learned that he had been arrested in the control room twice for passing bad checks. Needless to say, that ended my inquiries—and my interest. A larger station in a big market did hire him shortly afterward—obviously having failed to check his references. I wonder how long it took for the station to regret it.

You should be aware that as the law is currently practiced, you can be sued for giving a current or former employee a bad reference. That the bad reference is true is a good defense—but you may have to go to court and pay a lot of legal fees to offer it, and you may still have to prove a lack of malice. Until tort reform of some sort, that's the way it is. So you see, I was lucky to get the degree of candor in that reference that I did.

When you check references, listen for "undercurrents" in what's said. Does the person seem to be choosing his or her words carefully? Does the person seem to lack enthusiasm, even though the words seem positive enough? If you aren't sure what you're being told, probe a little: Would you hire him again? What are the applicant's weak points? Has she ever disappointed you or embarrassed you? How does the applicant work with others? Listen not only to the words but to the underlying emotional content of the reply you receive. You can't rely on what's said to you as being absolutely truthful, but a reference check is a must.

By the way, if the reference listed on a résumé fails to give a good recommendation for the applicant, you have to wonder why. Did the applicant fail to get permission before listing the reference? If the reference can't recall the person you're asking about, that's probably what happened, and you should then wonder about how detail-oriented or responsible the applicant really is.

Of course, a bad reference can be malicious and untrue. However, if it is a bad reference, you are justified in presuming that the applicant had no better reference to offer and was hoping that you wouldn't check; avoid hiring this person. The best way to deal with a problem employee is not to hire them in the first place.

Helping the New Hire Settle In

Once you've made the hire, help the person get settled in your town if he or she has moved. This is the scariest part of a new job; the new hire is vulnerable and has many more questions than answers. Some help and kindness at the outset can yield loyalty and cooperation later on.

If the new hire needs some money to complete the move, I would counsel against a personal loan. Loaning money from your own pocket puts you in an awkward position with the new hire from the start. If you let the debt recede into the background, so to speak, to avoid a debtor-creditor relationship with the employee when you need to be a mentor, you run a big risk of not getting repaid, even if the person really intends to do it. Instead, with your general manager's help, set up an advance on salary. Have the new hire sign an agreement to repay the station through specified paycheck deductions.

After your new hires meet the staff and get some orientation about the market, they should receive a copy of the format book. Give them time to read through it more than once. Advise them to listen to the station, trying to anticipate what will happen next according to the handbook—and at what times, in what words, and so on. If your airstaff is following your station pattern as they should, this will help new hires learn and understand what to do.

Counsel new hires that when a question arises, they should first check the handbook to see if they can find the answer themselves. If they can't find the answer, they should sit down with you. (This will provide insights into the parts of the handbook that need more clarity or detail.) Tell new hires to keep the format book handy during their first few shifts and to use the index to find the answers they need, but also encourage them to call you with questions, if necessary, while they're on the air.

Never listen to a new hire's first shift on the air. The first shift will always be considerably less than perfect, and you'll be almost irresistibly drawn to butt in with comments and suggestions. You may choose to tell new hires that you won't listen to their first few shifts; this can ease the almost overwhelming pressure on them to make a good first impression and will allow them to get comfortable with what's demanded of them before they are judged on how they execute it.

Because new hires almost always make mistakes on the first shift or two—sometimes bad mistakes—I like to break in new hires on an all-night shift. If your station is on the air between midnight and dawn, you can debut new employees there for part of—and then all of—a shift. Pay the regular on-air person to be available nearby to offer help when necessary.

If your station signs off at midnight, consider signing it back on at 1 A.M. and operating it until an hour before the usual sign-on time to allow the new hire to practice in a real on-air situation when few people are likely to be listening. (Somebody will have to be there to offer help when needed—preferably not you, so there isn't the pressure of the boss lurking outside.)

With your new on-air people comfortable on the air and working their assigned shift, it's time to start listening to them in depth—and to start offering comments after their shift is over. Give them some positive feedback every time at this point, complimenting them on what they're doing that you like and the good progress that you've noted. Then bring up any points that need work. This provides context for the criticism.

The context is important because on-air people are performers, and they place their egos—the essence of who they are as people—out in front of everyone when they're on the air. They tend to take criticism of what they do as criticism of their competence and of themselves as people if the context of the critique is not established—and that can destroy their self-confidence and performance. "Making something good even better" is a much more positive way to present criticism rather than blunt "suggestions for improvement," even if their performance badly needs improvement.

When their performance is acceptable, begin a regular process of meeting individually with all of your on-air people to listen to one of their airchecks together. These critique sessions will let you hone and fine-tune their work—provided that you continue to set the context by praising that which is good. If employees are scared to go into a critique session with you, either you've made a bad hire and they know they can't perform to your expectations, or you are not setting the context and all they get from you is pickiness and negative comments. Either way, they'll soon be looking for another job, even if you want them to stay.

Some PDs prefer to have a monthly critique session in which the whole airstaff gets together and interacts as their airchecks are played. If you have a tight and accomplished team with no self-confidence problems, this may work, but it can also result in a cliquish and destructive atmosphere and a loss of self-confidence by some of your airstaff. If you are considering this approach, try it once to see how it goes, and get feedback from the participants individually before making it an established policy.

Your goal is to have a motivated, tight team of pros going out and winning for you. Your method of motivation and direction must be selected and practiced to accomplish this.

Developing Air Talent

Let's conclude this chapter with some tips about directing and developing air talent. To start with, be clear in your own mind about the criteria you use in selecting your airstaff and the specific performance you expect from them. This is important because different program directors place their priorities on very different attributes. Many PDs hire primarily for voice or delivery; others are more interested in uniqueness of thought or expression and creativity.

The single most important thing I look for in an on-air person is the ability to relate personally and individually with the listener, so I hire intelligent and lively minds. That's what personality really is; it's not humor, unless it's naturally part of one's thinking and self-expression. When a station has interesting and engaging individuals on the air who can relate to the listener one-to-one, their delivery is much less important and can be developed on the job. For me, an on-air person must be a human being first.

A warning about working with creative people: The stronger the personalities of your on-air people, the more difficult it is to be their boss. These people are not sheep. The liner-card-reader type tends to be bland and cooperative, though a nonentity on the air, whereas somebody with a mind is always going to be harder to work with. You'd better decide what you value and the effort you're willing to invest to attain it with your staff.

If you seek to develop your airstaff as personalities, you will no doubt want to encourage them to ad-lib. The essential thing to understand about ad-libbing on radio is that it should never be done without knowing what the point of the remark is. You've undoubtedly heard someone get "trapped" in a thought on the air and talk around and around it, trying to figure out how to get out. When you hear that, you've heard someone who started talking before knowing what his or her point was. Unfortunately, you may sometimes hear that happen even in top markets. It's unprofessional.

Impress on your airstaff not only to what degree you permit ad-libbing, but also that it's mandatory that before they start talking about something, they must know the point of what they're planning to say. Then they should get to it as directly as possible. If they can't figure out the point of a planned comment, obviously they shouldn't even start it. As long as they do have a point and get to it directly, the listener will not be running a stopwatch on the comment and will not consider it too long no matter how long it lasts. However, an irrelevant and pointless remark of even just ten seconds will grate on the listener and seem like too much talk.

A real problem for air talent, particularly in smaller markets but sometimes at higher levels, too, is sounding like an announcer. When we first got into radio, we thought we were supposed to sound like announcers. Wrong! The goal is *not* to sound like one.

You see, the listener cannot relate to someone with an "announcer delivery"—they can only identify with an interesting person. Does this mean that air talent today are better off without technique? Emphatically not. On the contrary, the techniques we learn as announcers must be learned so well that the listener doesn't notice them as they enhance our communicating abilities.

Consider this analogy: If we go to a high school music recital and young Johnny gets up to play his violin solo, he may do a very creditable job, but both he and the audience are painfully aware of his efforts to play well. The audience sits tensely, hoping he won't hit a sour note. On the other hand, when Yehudi Menuhin or another master of the violin plays, superb technique is certainly on display, but it's so much a natural part of the performer and seems so effortless that we only hear the great music. We never notice the technique at all.

In radio on-air work, the same is true. The great pros in the business do have good diction, great breath control, fine mike technique, and the ability to be perceived as a real human being at any time—and we never notice the superb technique used to accomplish this. The goal in radio is to have such professionalism, such technique, that you communicate superbly as a person and don't sound like an announcer.

What do you do if you have an on-air person who sounds fine when you chat with him or her but who turns on the mike and sounds mechanical or artificial? A helpful idea from the great radio personality Casey Kasem is to record some of his or her spots or breaks and splice them together, back-to-back without interruption, and then let the on-air person hear the monotonous result.

If this technique doesn't work, you might try having your air talent imagine, when on the air, that somebody they know is sitting right across from them—but behind a curtain—listening. Would they then talk the same way they always announce if speaking to a friend in person? With good technique, they could and should.

Maybe you'll come up with another approach to the problem that works better than either of these! An accomplished announcing style is as much a matter of attitude as skill.

Breath Control

One skill that nearly all major-market air talents possess and that generally must be mastered by all on-air people before they can make the "big leagues" is breath control—sometimes called "projection" or "breathing from the diaphragm." If your airstaff hasn't mastered this skill, you can help them do it, and they—and your station—will sound much more professional.

Of course, we can't breathe *without* using the diaphragm because we have no muscles in our lungs. Lungs are simply limp sacs, and we fill them with air—breathe in—by pushing down the broad muscle called the diaphragm, which forms the bottom of the chest cavity. When the diaphragm moves down, like a piston descending within the cylinder of an engine, it creates a slight vacuum in the chest, which causes air to rush into and inflate the lungs. When the diaphragm moves back up, as a piston moves up in an engine's cylinder, it compresses the air in front of it. Air is pushed out of the lungs by this compression in the chest. Breathing is thus the result of having a sealed chest cavity.

The diaphragm is unique in the body. This muscle is subject to conscious control, but when not consciously controlled, it reverts to continuous, permanent automatic operation. We breathe without thinking about it, but we can control and discipline our breathing to accomplish what we want with our voice.

What kind of breath control are we talking about here? Stage performers usually learn breath control because they must. In the theater, actors play to a huge house full of seats, and they must be heard clearly all the way to the back wall—but without sounding like they are shouting. This calls for exceptional pronunciation and loud volume without changing the voice pitch. This is done by using lots of air.

Singers, if they hope for a long career, have to master the same skill. The late Janis Joplin demonstrated that one can sing loudly without this skill, but the result was pain and damage to the vocal chords, which she anesthetized with alcohol. That eventually led to her death—the ultimate price for her lack of proper breath control.

In small markets, radio announcers can often get by without using their breath correctly, but they tend to sound thin and reedy on the air and perhaps rather nasal, often with slurred pronunciation or swallowed words. They won't advance.

I've found that the biggest impediment in learning how to use breath correctly is not knowing what it feels like to do so. I tried to learn the technique for years without success—until I caused enough pain to my vocal chords that I stumbled onto the correct technique by accident in trying to ease the discomfort in my throat. Once I knew what it felt like to breathe properly, I was able to do it without problems.

Here's an exercise to help announcers understand what the proper use of the breath feels like. I've written the instructions that follow directly to the person trying to master the technique, to make it easier for you to use the text as a tool to help your staff members learn proper breath control. When you use this part of the book to guide your airstaff into proper breath use, you'll be delighted with the result on the air and with the new proficiency and confidence shown by your staff.

1. Begin by taking a deep breath and holding it. You'll notice that you're plugging your airway at the back of your throat with your uvula. Unblock your airway without letting any of the air out. Surprise! You can do it.
2. Slowly let the air out about halfway, and then slowly breathe all the way back in, and hold it again—all without physically blocking the airway at the back of the throat. (Legal notice: Resume normal breathing now while I explain what just happened.)

Most people suppose that the only way they can hold a deep breath is by plugging up the airway in the back of their throat, and they believe that if and when they release that deep breath, it will all whoosh out at once, as if releasing the neck of an inflated balloon. Of course, you *can* let the air out like that—if you want—but you don't have to. What actually holds the air in is simply the diaphragm remaining in the "down" position. Your airway can be completely open, then, and the air will stay in when you want it to.

You see, the diaphragm is a muscle we use from the moment we are born. It's now already fully developed and needs no special exercise to use it the way we must in radio. We can control it perfectly the first time we try. It's just that up to this point, we didn't know what to do or how to do it. There's really nothing more to it than that.

Let's apply breath control to speaking. Our vocal chords create our voice, but the raw material of voice is air. The more passing air that the vocal chords can use to make sound, the easier they can do it and the more control and mastery you have of the result.

Simply get in the habit of taking a deep breath before speaking. Not just speaking in front of a microphone, but speaking anywhere, in front of anyone: in person, on the phone, and on the radio. Then, when you're talking, release just as much air as needed to speak effortlessly. (Don't blow it all out at once in a windy gust.)

When you're speaking, a significant amount of air should be coming out of your mouth. When you're momentarily silent, your mouth may still be open with your airway unblocked. Keep your diaphragm in position so that no air flows at that moment. Then, speak again and resume exhaling.

As for "reloading"—taking the next deep breath—don't suck it in through your nose. That's noisy and takes too long. With your mouth slightly open, push your diaphragm down quickly. In an instant, your lungs are again full. This can be done between sentences—even in the middle of a sentence if needed. Inhaling in this way is not noisy, so it won't be noticeable to the listener.

When you use enough air in speaking, the result is that you can and should relax the throat muscles. Throat strain goes completely away, even when you are speaking loudly and keeping your voice tone in the normal range. Speaking, and getting the voice effect you want, becomes effortless. You feel really in control of how you come across for the first time. It's a great feeling.

How are you doing? If you aren't using enough air as you speak, your throat will still feel somewhat tight and tense. It shouldn't. It should feel—and be—completely relaxed.

Incidentally, your voice tone drops a bit and sounds fuller and more resonant when you are breathing correctly. The tighter the string on a guitar or in a piano, the higher the pitch. When you relax your throat muscles, the "strings" you speak with get looser and drop to their normal pitch—a pitch you may never have used before.

Never try to force your voice tone lower than its natural pitch for speaking, though—that can really strain your throat and cause permanent problems. When your throat is relaxed and your vocal chords are just modulating the strong passing air propelled by your diaphragm and deep breathing, you will for the first time be using your normal and natural voice tone, and it will sound great.

Now that you know what good breath use in speaking feels like, all that's left to do is to practice until it becomes a habit. Set aside fifteen to thirty minutes a day for reading aloud from a book or magazine using proper breath techniques, as described here. Practice these techniques every time you speak, even when chatting with friends in person or speaking on the phone. Speak naturally, not like an "announcer."

The more you discipline yourself to do this all the time, the faster it will become a habit, requiring no conscious control from you. You'll have mastered an essential skill that you must have to open the doors of large markets. You may feel strange using this technique in front of people for a while, but there will be no amused reaction like the one you'd get if you were sounding like an "announcer." In fact, you'll just sound like *you*—only better than ever before. Try it.

Some program directors deliberately avoid hiring people with real talent out of fear that they'll be moving on to bigger markets before long. That's foolish. If you can't pay big-market money, you probably can't keep major-league talents "on the way up," but if you treat them well, you'll hold them longer than you expect because they'll only leave for an offer they can't pass up.

Hiring the big-league radio talents of tomorrow builds your station a reputation for being a great place for developing talent and moving to the big markets. It also builds you a reputation for being a great talent-developing program director. The result is that the best and the brightest of the upcoming talents (along with a lot of the wanna-bes who won't make the cut) will be trying to get onto your staff and work with you. It's not a bad position in which to find yourself.

5

Music as a Programming Weapon

Using Music Strategically

For most radio stations, the primary programming product is music. Generally, the music is of a specific type, played consistently—a music format. Many program directors believe that all stations in their format play the same music, and thus they put little effort into selecting the songs they play. They believe that it's what surrounds the music that makes the station distinctive, and they all too often simply follow the charts to select music—perhaps waiting until a song is an established hit before playing it, to minimize the risk of making bad choices.

Yes, as discussed in previous chapters, the individual elements of a station's presentation *are* critical to the establishment of its identity to its listeners, and these elements deserve the closest thought and attention to detail. However, it is foolish not to devote the same effort to selecting the music because it is the single most predominant programming element of such stations—and the primary reason the listener tunes in.

The programmer who prefers to wait for hits to become established before playing them is rationalizing as follows: (1) I don't know what my listeners really like of the new and current music, so I'll wait for others to determine that, and (2) my listeners want "familiarity" in the music, which means limiting the exposure of new songs and emphasizing older ones.

In reality, the only stations that can really be confident that what their listeners want is noncurrent music are the Oldies stations, including Classic Rock stations, and stations that concentrate on a past decade or era. Putting those aside for the time being, stations for which current music has relevance are exceedingly foolish if they don't make current music part of their winning strategy.

If noncurrent music really were what most listeners wanted to hear, then Oldies-type stations would always beat stations that are not as closely identified with older music. In fact, though, most music listeners choose stations without a nostalgia connection specifically because they are more interested in today and tomorrow than wallowing in yesterday. So, overdoing the familiarity angle with a current music station fails to meet the needs and expectations of the station's listeners and narrows the distinction between the station and its Oldies competitors. Familiarity is simply a comfort factor and is no more important than other relevant factors for current-music stations.

Inasmuch as all of today's music formats owe their origin to the development of Top 40, let's concentrate on that format in our discussion. From there we'll explore the directions in which the subsequent format offshoots (Country, Adult Contemporary, Urban, and so on) must go to maximize their appeal.

The basic principle of Top 40 has always been to determine what today's "average" pop music listeners want and to give it to them in a repeating pattern. The source of all current pop music is always the youth, who constantly seek to define themselves through new music forms, distinct from the music with which adults are comfortable.

From the beginning, Top 40 successfully based its playlist on the sales of recorded songs in the form of singles—as opposed to albums, where what motivated the sale cannot usually be traced to a particular song—and on listener requests. Both are areas in which youths dominate, although there will always be some adults who listen to Top 40 to "keep up with the pop culture" even if they don't like many of the songs.

Top 40 has always thrived on the unexpectedness of what would catch the public fancy. Top 40 stations today that ignore hit songs that "don't fit" the station, such as ballads by standard artists, novelty records, and pop instrumentals (such as movie themes), leave out what often is the most attractive element of real Top 40 to the audience they seek.

I should add, though, that Top 40 stations, and stations in other music formats, should omit records that are not hits with their audience, regardless of chart status. With the rise of trade charts in the early nineties based on measured sales, format distinctions in hit charts tended to disappear. Records that would not have made the Top 40 charts in previous years because record stores would not have reported these sales to Top 40 stations, having seen that these songs weren't selling to Top 40 listeners, now did so. Many rap records, selling hugely in the nineties, but not to listeners of mainstream Top 40 stations, were played on Top 40 stations as a result—adversely affecting Top 40 ratings.

It's dangerous to think that undiscriminating sales tallies can translate to viable Top 40 playlists, and it's even more dangerous to routinely make snap decisions rejecting hit records in order to tailor the sound of the station. A Top 40 station that has a consistent, tailored music identity is no longer in the Top 40 format but has a niche format for a specific audience—usually, a smaller audience. Programmers in all formats must be ever more diligent in finding exactly what their audiences like and what they don't.

In addition, an element of surprise is a legitimate part of all current-music-based formats. Listeners are never entirely predictable in their preferences, and kids and adults alike do enjoy surprise and novelty in their music from time to time.

Returning to the rationale described at the beginning of this chapter, though: If you make the majority of your "music add" choices based on avoiding risk, you are playing defense. You know what they say about that: You never win playing defense. (They also say that a good offense is the best defense.)

Because listeners tune in non-Oldies formats specifically because they like to hear new records, you'd better be playing some if you program a non-Oldies station—and not just the "safe," proven ones either. In any business—and radio is no exception—without risk there can be no gain. Of course, the risk must be calculated and intelligently considered, but risks must be taken if you are to achieve competitive advantage.

As I wrote January 14, 1994, in my "PD Notebook" column in *Gavin*, the radio programming magazine published weekly in San Francisco:

Let me say here that if you throw caution to the wind and add all sorts of risky records, you'll go down in flames. Intelligent risk-taking means knowing what you're doing. But a program director taking intelligent risks will be aware that in most pop formats, the song is more important than the artist, and he or she will put aside "automatic adds" for songs by familiar artists, and instead listen for the unusual, offbeat and catchy song—even if it's by an unknown artist.

An intelligent program director understands that being different has less risk, competitively, that being the same as everybody else. And though nobody likes to receive negative calls about a song, a program director should understand that songs which can arouse positive emotions in some listeners are capable of arousing negative emotions in others. If you don't get a few negative calls about a record now and then, you probably aren't getting anybody's attention, and you're vulnerable to competition.

Here's that fundamental programming truth again: The only reason listeners tune in your station is the expectation of what they will hear. Those expectations are usually based on past experiences with the station. If there's no contrast and variety in your music, and you're relying entirely on delivering a generic product, you are—again—vulnerable to competition.

To build positive listener expectations about your music, you must first define your limits—how far from the "center" of your format you can go— and include all records within this boundary for airplay consideration. Next, you must build meaningful music categories, and find a way to allow the listener to sense the difference between those categories, by the way you juxtapose them, even if they don't recognize the difference consciously. Then you must work out a predictable playlist sequence to deliver consistent variety within those limits.

This variety defines your station's musical approach and builds listener expectations about the music they'll hear when they tune in. Don't overlook the power of a well-chosen new record—newness is as appealing to adults as it is to teens. The important part is identifying which of the new records will do the job for you. When making this choice, be aware that your fellow program directors are more likely to be selecting records primarily for "safety" than potential "appeal," so consensus adds in the trade magazines may not always be the right songs to maximize appeal to your audience.

Steer away from having lots of music categories, and an extended sequence of categories, which is a great temptation with modern computer playlisting. The average listener only tunes in 15 to 30 minutes per day (although the median listening spans reported by the rating services are considerably longer, stretched by a handful of listeners who tune in for hours every day). Thus, if you don't substantially complete your category sequence in 15 to 20 minutes, you run an unnecessary risk of seeming musically inconsistent to the majority of your listeners as they tune in at random times in the hour. That reduces expectations, and decreases listeners' frequency of listening, and their listening spans.

One final thought: Stations which allow their airstaff to rearrange scheduled records within the hour experience the loss of "category juxtaposition," and are causing reduced listener expectations of their music.

This excerpt provides the philosophical underpinning for this chapter. But wait! How do we do all this?

Identifying Listener Preferences

For Top 40 radio, recorded music sales and station requests are still quite valid as programming tools. However, as noted, you'll have to be careful to establish that it *is* your current or potential audience that's buying the music. Requests can help pinpoint album tracks that you should consider, as well as give you an idea of how long to play a particular song: If it remains a top request for months, it may warrant strong airplay for months, even if other stations dropped it long ago.

Requests tend to be from the young end of the audience, and they are definitely subject to "hyping"—repeat requests from the same person or group of people. This must be taken into consideration, and when multiple "votes" by the same person are noted, they should be discounted. However, hyping by a group of people can occasionally alert you to a hot new artist with a fan club. "Artist values" tend to be more important for teens than for any other group of listeners. Even then, the song is more important than the artist in determining airplay.

In my observation, artist values may be of most importance to the eighteen- to twenty-four-year-old listener. Listeners of this age have rejected both the teen culture and the values of their parents, and they seek to establish their individuality through eclecticism; this is especially true of men in this age group. However, because of the motivation just described for this listener group, programming primarily to the eighteen- to twenty-four-year-old young man invariably destroys the broader pop appeal of any station.

In any pop format, be alert to hot new trends in the pop culture (movies, artists, songs, fads, etc.). Find a way to reflect them on the air if relevant to your audience.

If your station is one of the offshoots of Top 40 and is oriented toward adults aged twenty-five and older, artist values decline farther in importance. Because these listeners tend not to be aggressive record buyers and seldom call to make a request (those who do are usually not typical of your audience as a whole), it's harder to establish what they like musically.

For a number of years, the most common way to determine adult preferences for new and current songs has been through "telephone callouts." This practice consists of randomly calling households in the station's metro and screening those reached to establish that only households whose tastes lean to the station's approach are included in this survey. Then the researcher plays "hooks" of the songs to be tested down the phone line to them, securing responses based on familiarity and preference for each one. A hook is the catchiest, most highly identifiable part of a song—often the chorus or refrain. I discussed the drawbacks of this method of testing in Chapter 3, and I refer you to that chapter for some thoughts on the requirements for good music research and some suggestions for alternate methodology.

A problem with hook-based research not mentioned earlier is that the person being tested cannot meaningfully respond to a fragment of a *new* song that they haven't heard before; the hook does not mean anything to them yet. Because new music is an essential ingredient of all contemporary pop music formats, some valid method of determining the audience's reaction to new and unfamiliar music must be developed and used.

As pointed out in Chapter 3, you must understand this important criterion of all music research and indeed all programming research: What you are trying to determine is behavior, not opinion. It's not impossible; I know a number of program directors who have come up with innovative, imaginative approaches that consistently get valuable results.

Using Noncurrent Music Strategically

Generally, whatever method you have chosen to test new and current music can also be adapted to test older music for acceptability. Be aware of a key difference between "currents" and "noncurrents," however: The currents represent the current tastes and status of the pop culture—or that part of it that your station is intended to reflect. Include the widest possible variety within your musical boundaries, but do not expect that most of it can or will be retained for later noncurrent airplay.

In a current-oriented format, the noncurrents—as I pointed out earlier—are the comfort factor. These songs provide the frame for the current music, making use of familiarity as a counterpoint to the newness of the current music. Just as with the currents, noncurrents should be selected for their appeal to your target audience.

However, there are two key differences. First, noncurrent songs define the mainstream of the format, so there should be more consistency in the sound of these songs and less variety than is desirable in the current playlist. Second, familiarity is the only reason to include noncurrent music, so the widespread familiarity of noncurrent songs to your target audience is even more important than how much they like them. (However, do not include songs that don't appeal at all to your audience just because they're familiar.)

Additionally, with the noncurrents it's important to probe beyond mere preference and familiarity. A song can be liked and familiar to your target audience and still be totally irrelevant to them. That would make the song a nostalgia piece and thus useful only for nostalgia-based (Oldies) formats. Too often, current-based stations inadvertently play noncurrents that only appeal for their nostalgia value—and so create the impression to the listener that they are some sort of Oldies station, instead of being properly perceived as the modern alternative to Oldies stations. This makes them unexpectedly vulnerable when Oldies competitors appear.

The distinction between these two types of noncurrents is important. The nostalgia noncurrent reminds the listener of times gone by. The sort of noncurrent needed for current-based stations is the one that the listener thinks of simply as a favorite song. It should not arouse listener associations with the era from which it came.

To illustrate: The Adult Contemporary audience usually thinks of the Beatles' "Yesterday" as a good song, rather than an old song. The same audience regards Tony Orlando's "Tie a Yellow Ribbon 'Round the Old Oak Tree" as a musical museum piece, even though it's a much more recent record, was an even bigger hit on the charts than "Yesterday," is still familiar, and may even be liked by some listeners.

Building a Playlist of Noncurrents

The next step in building a playlist for your station, whether it's a current music or oldies-based format, is to define how far back in time your noncurrents should go. This is usually determined by the younger end of the target audience you seek because the younger the listeners, the more important they consider the music selected and played. Conversely, because the noncurrents rely on familiarity, do not include any noncurrents that will not be familiar to your younger in-target listeners.

Set a cutoff year for the noncurrents. For general purposes, determine when the younger end of your target audience was in its early to mid-teens, and use this as your cutoff point. You can make exceptions for songs that are so widely familiar that even the younger end of your target demographic group will know and like them. For today's Adult Contemporary format, "Yesterday" might be an example of such an unusual timeless song even though it predates the birth of the younger end of the format's target audience.

Next, consider whether listeners will regard each song as a good song or an old one. For a current-oriented format, omit the nostalgia items. For a nostalgia-based format, the reverse would be true, and surprisingly, you probably shouldn't automatically rule out current material in an oldies format. While working as program director at a San Francisco station in the early nineties, my friend Jason W. Fine demonstrated very successfully that some currents can work in a fifties/sixties-based rock-and-roll format. He chose suitable current remakes, and new songs by artists associated with the key era, and he obtained good ratings. His innovative idea put an element of freshness into a nostalgia format.

It is extremely important when putting together a noncurrent playlist to consider every single song using the criteria you've chosen. Playlists rapidly deteriorate when you let yourself think, "This one is pretty marginal, but I like it, and after all, it's just one among so many." It is essential that every individual song fully meets your criteria. This is important when putting together a playlist of current songs too. You'll play nothing but strong music if every song has to meet your criteria to make the playlist, and in today's competitive environment, you cannot compete with anything less.

Sidestepping a Noncurrent Trap

When forming noncurrent categories, it has become standard practice to determine through research the four, six, or eight hundred "most preferred" songs—and then play just those. This is a trap that can lead to a likable but ultimately really boring radio station. Here's a parallel: It's possible in Top 40 radio to determine the five strongest currents at any given time, but stations fail if they play only those. Instead, successful stations stress the top songs but play the other, lesser currents too, in a lower rotation, for variety and balance. The same reasoning should apply to all noncurrent music, too.

Do determine those few hundred most popular noncurrents for your target audience, and put them in a high rotation so that they repeat often; but augment them with a wide variety of other noncurrents that also meet your criteria, and play these at a much lower rotation. If the high-stress songs repeat every four days, the low-stress ones may repeat every three or four weeks. The lower-stress categories should appear less often in the hour, too. With a larger library of songs feeding these lesser categories, you can achieve this lower rotation.

The result, then, is a high degree of overall preference and familiarity but with those low-rotation noncurrents giving the station an amazing feeling of variety, low repetition, and depth of library. There is no format that will not benefit by this rather obvious, but completely "unfashionable" approach!

Categorizing and Creating a Sequence

Once you have determined which current and noncurrent songs to play, segment them into meaningful categories, making sure that the distinctions you use would be meaningful to the listener and that you use as few categories as possible. This will assist you in minimizing the number of minutes needed to complete your music category sequence, thus keeping the station consistent to listeners who tune in at random times and listen for short periods.

Here's the type of thinking that should go into creating your categories. If you have identified those top few hundred best-liked noncurrents for your target audience, you can group them in one category—let's call it A. Then I suggest you build a B list of secondary noncurrents for low rotation. Fifteen hundred is not an excessive number of songs for this category, and even more can be included if each and every song fully meets your criteria for making the list. If the B category spans two or three decades, you might decide to break it into two categories—earlier songs (C) and more recent ones (B)—to ensure an "era balance."

Then, the current playlist might be broken down into the strongest hits (the Y songs), and the secondary ones, which are on their way up or down (the Zs). That gives us enough categories to create a very basic four-record sequence. For example:

> [Start of hour]
> A
> Y
> Alternate B and C
> Z
> [Repeat sequence to end of hour]

In this example, the goal is to achieve a consistent balance of music, creating a subliminal pattern that the listener will grow to understand and expect—thus promoting both tune-in and repeat or extended listening. If this pattern is completed and restarted in 15 minutes of time or so, the station will seem to meet listener expectations, no matter when they tune in or how long they listen. I strongly suggest that you not develop a category sequence longer than about five records because it would take longer to complete than the station's mean listening span!

If you do need more time for your sequence, you can alternate categories within a single position in the rotation, as done with categories B and C in the preceding example. Be sure, though, that the categories being rotated in a single position have an equivalent, compatible effect on the listener within the full sequence.

You'll notice, by the way, that the format used in this example is a song *sequence*. There is a tradition in radio of using a "clock" for music rotation, with the categories displayed as pie-shaped wedges on the hourly clock. I don't like such clocks because odd-length records throw them off. To stay on the prescribed sequence, the air talent either has to move the spot breaks from where they're supposed to be or has to drop records. Both of these adjustments can upset listener expectations.

If you choose to use a repeating sequence, as in this example, the music balance will be maintained throughout each hour regardless of song length and spot load. The spot breaks go at fixed places shown on the program log, placed at the end of whichever song in the sequence is nearest to the indicated break time. The airstaff, then, is able to meet the specified times for breaks and still maintain the music consistency of the station at all times in the hour.

Once you've gotten the music rotating consistently, with songs rotating evenly within their categories, you may want to refine the result by adding "screens," or rules by which the optimum song to play next in each category is identified by a computer or by your on-air people. A tempo screen, for example, might prohibit two slow records in a row in the sequence. An artist screen might prohibit the same artist from appearing twice in an hour. With modern computer playlisting, you can add any number of screens. To make sure that songs rotate as evenly as possible, I suggest that you keep the screens to a minimum, ensuring that each one makes a meaningful music-balance distinction perceptible to the listener. Otherwise the computer will skip too many records and unnecessarily shorten your rotations.

Incidentally, a thought about computer playlists: I myself have worked with a preselected, computerized playlist paired with a prepared program log, which I found left the air talent out of every phase of the programming selection process, making the on-air shift very boring for an intelligent "personality," leading to weak content in the breaks. Not enough thinking is required when everything is preselected!

I find that I get more out of air talent if they have a hand in selecting the music, even if from very limited choices. For that reason, I still like the use of filing-card music rotation systems, with one song per card and one box of cards per category. (Take a card from the front, and replace it in the back of the box.) In such cases, I have two or three mandatory criteria: The tempo and genre of songs must vary within a sequence. I instruct air talent to select the song at the front of each category, unless it doesn't meet the specified criteria. Then the air talent is to dig down into the category no more than three or four titles to find a better choice (and never intentionally avoid any songs altogether).

I've been asked whether such procedure isn't an invitation for the airstaff to "cheat" and skew the music in some direction or other. I have never found this to happen if the rules I've specified are followed. If I found I couldn't trust someone to follow these simple rules, I'd have to replace him or her.

If you prefer computer playlisting—and there certainly are a lot of computerized music-scheduling programs available—I suggest choosing one that involves the on-air person in music selection. Specifically, the program should offer the on-air person a choice of two or three titles for the next category scheduled. Give your airstaff a few simple rules to achieve the best balance, and let them select the next song from the limited choices offered. Don't let the computer discard a choice that is not selected; it must keep offering it as an option until it is used.

Determining the Length of a Current-Music Playlist

When I was discussing playlisting noncurrents, you'll notice I presented them in terms of how often the average record would rotate, or repeat, rather than an arbitrary number of songs. That, again, is a listener-oriented criterion—as all programming decisions must be. For the playlist of currents, the length of the list should be determined by the desired rotation and by nothing else. Specifically, you must determine how often the current records should repeat. Bear in mind that you're playing these because your listeners like them, and in a current-based format, they serve as a metaphor for the current state of society or culture.

Listeners want to hear the songs they like with some frequency. If you play their favorites too seldom, listeners won't hear them enough to expect that you'll play them again. This discourages repeat and long-span listening. On the other hand, if you play these songs too often, they might seem repetitive to listeners and cause them to tune out too quickly, shortening listening spans.

In general, the younger the target audience, the more often the current hits should rotate. In Top 40, the top hits may rotate as often as every hour and a quarter! These are the songs that young people tune in to hear. They represent "today." In Adult Contemporary, however, two and a half to three hours might be more suitable for the high rotation.

To understand how playlist length relates to rotation, let's go back to that four-category sequence proposed earlier, and let's assume it's for an Adult Contemporary format. We decide that we want a primary rotation of two and a half hours for current hits and a secondary rotation of six hours for less popular current hits.

In this example, I purposely did not choose five hours for the length of the secondary rotation because that would mean that every two rotations of the two-and-a-half-hour "high rotation" list would synchronize with the same songs on the five-hour "secondary" list—far too predictable. In twenty-four hours of broadcasting, the two-and-a-half-hour list will be repeated 9.6 times (24 divided by 2.5), while the six-hour list will be repeated four times (24 divided by 6). The two lists will stay out of synchronization for days on end.

We're getting close now to figuring out how many records should be in each current category. First, we must determine how many songs will be played in the average hour. Let's say it averages out to sixteen. This means that a four-song sequence is completed exactly four times in the average hour (16 divided by 4 equals 4).

So, on average, the high-rotation hits would be played four times an hour, and the low-rotation hits would also be played four times an hour. If there are four high-rotation records per hour, how many are played in a desired repeat pattern of two and a half hours? 2.5 times 4 is 10, so the high-rotation list should be ten songs long.

There will also be four low-rotation currents per hour, and we want a six-hour repeat pattern for these. We multiply six hours times four songs per hour, and that equals twenty-four songs. The total current playlist of songs, in both rotations, then turns out to be 34 records.

If you lock your playlist at the exact number of songs you chose using this method, rather than let it vary slightly in quantity from week to week, you'll find this not only maintains the integrity of your rotation pattern, but it gives you great discipline. You see, if you have to take one song off the list to add a new song, you must consciously determine if the new song is as strong as the one you must take off. This should help you avoid adding borderline, weak records.

A parting word about your music selections: It's admirable to be a music connoisseur and to want to expose "excellent" music and to avoid banal tunes, but unless you work for a noncommercial station and can afford to be elitist, this would be a very bad mistake. This is known as "being too hip for the room," and an amazing number of program directors are guilty of it to some degree. Don't fall into this trap.

As a program director, part of your job is to get into the mind of, and to be comfortable with the tastes of, your target listener. Another programming friend of mine, Bobby Irwin, who specializes in Adult Contemporary (A/C) formats, has an interesting technique. The A/C format is female-based, and his target listener is in her thirties. He gives her a name (Darlene) and, after researching the core of his audience, outlines every meaningful element of her life. He specifies her age, defines her concerns, and even identifies her family members and their ages. Then he determines what her tastes would be in an amazing number of categories, and he communicates all these to his staff and asks them to talk specifically to Darlene. Irwin keeps up-to-date with Darlene's world by watching TV programs that might appeal to her, by reading her magazines, and by staying on her wavelength in every way he can.

Of course, a great many of the station's listeners must necessarily be profoundly different from "Darlene" or whoever this hypothetical individual listener may be. However, if your airstaff identifies with a listener who represents "the heart of the target," thus visualizing the typical listener, they are far ahead of most competing stations in identifying with and programming to their target audience. If you cannot define your target listener as specifically as Bobby Irwin does, you probably don't have a clear idea of the people for whom you're programming. You had better find out.

6

News as a Programming Weapon

At one time, the rules of the Federal Communications Commission (FCC) required every station to broadcast a minimum quantity of news. When this obligation was lifted during the deregulation period of the early eighties, many program directors of music-oriented stations breathed a sigh of relief and did away with most (or all) newscasts. Today, any remaining news broadcasts are usually restricted to the morning show, and in-depth or consistent news coverage is left to the All-News, News-Talk, or self-styled "full-service" radio stations. This can be a serious mistake.

The first step in deciding how much news your station should be presenting is to rethink the old cliché that news is a "tune-out." Certainly, the FCC's previous mandate for newscasts resulted in a lot of boring and dull news broadcasts, and these were indeed tune-outs, but news can be interesting. In fact, by definition, news *is* interesting—that's what makes it "news."

In this chapter, I'll discuss general principles and approaches to radio news that apply to all stations that use news in any way. When these principles are applied to short, regular newscasts on a music station, news can actually be an audience attractor. It is one of the most potent ways of relating a station to its community. Thus it is one of the strongest tools that a station can use to remain relevant in an era in which much of the rest of the station "package"—be it music or some form of talk—can be approximated if not duplicated by a big-budget national broadcast service delivered by satellite, automation, or other means.

The Number One Audience Expectation of Radio News

To begin, let's develop a yardstick by which to measure the effectiveness of news on a radio station. Painful as it is to those of us who know exactly how well, how objectively, and how thoroughly radio can cover any story, public opinion surveys never rank radio high as a primary source of news. Television usually comes first, and even newspapers are usually cited ahead of radio. Only the weekly newsmagazines rank below radio as a primary source of news for the public.

However, with additional probing, an important role for radio emerges. When the public is asked to rank news sources in the order in which they expect to learn *first* about news events, radio is number one. Television is number two, and all other sources follow. This being the case, it is remarkable that so few people in radio, even at All-News stations, fully understand how best to meet listener expectations of radio news. Forming and meeting listener expectations is the essence of all successful radio programming, as explained earlier in this book.

Disappointingly, the few radio stations that do attempt to provide consistent news service around the clock today seem to regard their newscasts as a franchise that requires little effort. The very fact that they are providing twenty-four-hour news, when most stations are not, seems to them to justify no more work than is necessary to fill up the available time with news. As a result, they rely too much on news wire copy and network news. If their local reporters go out on stories, more often than not they are sent to planned media events and scheduled civic meetings.

This is the sort of thing that TV news has relied on in the past. Because television emphasizes pictures, the cameras are dispatched to wherever usable news pictures are most likely to be obtained. Today, however, with electronic news-gathering (ENG) techniques, television is changing—trying to become as immediate as the public expects radio to be. The ENG of TV news departments now not only includes quickly dispatched satellite trucks, but even transmission of slow-scanned pictorial news footage back to the TV station via tedious, lengthy feeds over conventional cellular and telephone lines. Thanks to aggressive TV newspeople, radio is in danger of losing the only news edge it has in the public's mind.

Your yardstick in determining whether the news coverage you offer on your station is effective and of value, no matter what your station's format, will have to be how well you meet the public's expectation that radio will be first with the significant news stories. Music stations that offer news coverage only in the mornings or only during morning and afternoon drive times cannot realistically expect that their listeners will ever tune to them for details of an important or breaking story. Their listeners won't be expecting them to cover breaking stories. Based on their past experience with the station, listeners already know that most of the time the station has no newscasts. They don't understand why morning or drive times are an exception. To them, it's just an inconsistency, and they have no clear idea of when the station may have news or, usually, what the station will cover in a newscast when one does occur.

Thus for music stations that only have news in the morning or during drive times, it would be wise to reposition the newscasts by calling them an "overnight update," "late afternoon final edition," or something similar. These newscasts are primarily designed to keep listeners who have been out of touch for a while sufficiently informed that they won't tune away to check the news elsewhere. The summary nature of these newscasts should be made clear so that listeners understand why the newscasts exist and just when they can expect to hear them. This can convert the news that is offered into a positive programming element.

No radio station can develop the image of "the radio station to turn to when news happens" if the news is not presented reliably around the clock. This should give a substantial advantage to the All-News stations, but many such stations today are simply headline services or headline-and-feature services, whose staffs think that they satisfy their news promise if they keep a routine news service going on the air hour after hour.

Because what listeners expect of a good radio news operation is immediacy, authority, and the ability to catch the breaking stories early, there is frequently an opportunity for a music station—or any other station not in an All-News format—to steal that image for themselves. The station must have some sort of newscast every hour at an established time to accomplish that, although the length of that newscast can vary according to content and time of day.

A strong news image is a competitive weapon for two reasons. The first is ratings: A strong news image can bring the station a bigger cumulative weekly audience. A strong news image will draw news listeners who don't normally listen to the station's music or regular format. It can improve audience shares, too, by bringing listeners who like to keep up to date on the news back to the station throughout the day.

The other advantage of a strong news image is building broader demographics; the extra news listeners you gain are often outside the station's normal age groups. Aggressive news coverage, locally oriented, will appeal to virtually all demographics. This is not just theory; I've seen the ratings. The elderly, who may not like the normal station format at all, will tune in for authoritative news. Believe it or not, even teens respond to news on their station (especially in the mornings)—although they will not tune into a station for news if the station does not appeal to them in its overall format.

The Composition of an Aggressive Newscast

On what sort of news should a station focus? An emphasis on legislative and scheduled news events may seem to be laudably nonsensational, but it can be boring for most listeners, and it offers no reason for any of them to tune into your station. On the other hand, nothing but crime and crisis news can be numbingly sensational. It would probably draw more audience than the more "dignified" approach of legislative and scheduled news events, but it still may not maximize audience. The solution is to combine the two, with special aggressiveness in reporting crime, emergency, and people-oriented news.

Aggressiveness is needed on those stories because they don't fall in your lap (or arrive in the mail) the way the dignified kinds of news may. In addition, even listeners who find the more sensational news unsettling or even deplorable will tend to judge your news effort by whether stories of this sort that they see later in the newspaper appeared first on your station; these tend to be the stories they remember. You downplay or ignore the visceral stories only at your peril.

Before moving on, a word about wire copy: The wire services, such as the Associated Press (AP), are valuable in providing coverage of areas outside your locality or primary focus. Don't assume, however, that you are necessarily being "early" with these news stories when they come from the news wire. AP, for example, is a co-op; members contribute news to it. Who do you suppose the biggest contributor is? Almost always, the major daily newspapers. Their membership means that they can print stories from the service; in return, their contribution consists, mostly, of allowing the wire service to rewrite and transmit the stories they've published.

Therefore, the wire service's stories from your area all too often happened a day or two ago, have already appeared in the paper, and only now are turning up on the radio. The newspapers love this situation, of course, because it puts them in the position of covering local news before radio does. With the time it takes newspapers to gather, write, publish, and distribute the news, there is no excuse for radio stations to be second with local stories, yet it's very common.

One way to resolve this problem is to use the newspaper stories simply as sources, and then go to the telephone and contact the principals in the story to ask the things that the newspapers didn't think to ask. The papers report what happened; radio can turn such stale news into fresh stories by asking: Why? What will happen next? What are the implications? How will this impact local residents?

In legislative stories, there is usually more than one side, and a story can be freshened by covering multiple points of view and the conflicts they represent. This process is highly recommended anyway, because it is usually a waste of time to assign a reporter to attend routine civic and legislative meetings. The newspapers cover them and routinely provide you with the facts you need to later update and freshen the stories for radio.

Freshening Old Stories and Finding New Stories

The sound bite or "actuality" (or the reporter's "voicer" from the scene) is the photograph of radio. Radio news is kept interesting, fresh, and immediate through these elements as long as the sound bite is important to the story, rather than included simply because of its easy availability. As a rule, never use audio cuts fed to you by partisans who are attempting to manage the news in their favor. Get the audio yourself or from an impartial source, such as the news department of a radio station in the locality where the story occurred.

You can regionalize your station by regularly trading voicers and actualities by telephone with stations elsewhere in your region. As long as you pay for the call and they get more or less equal reports from you, most stations are happy to engage in such trading. If the station gives you a voicer, though, make sure that they know what your established "news tag" or "station lockout phrase" is and that they end the voicer with it for you (for example, "This is John Doe in Allentown for WXXX News"; whatever phrase your station uses should be exactly the same wording each time).

Sources of News

As discussed above, the news wire and the key local and regional daily newspapers can provide you with leads for stories to update for radio. What are some of the other sources of news available to your aggressive news department?

Emergency Radio Services

First and foremost is the local police/fire/emergency radio services. You should have a scanner receiver in the newsroom monitoring these frequencies continuously, and it should be turned up loud enough so that somebody on the staff can hear it at all times. This will alert you to breaking news, local emergencies, traffic accidents, and so forth. Most of the time though, you should call the agency transmitting the report for details before broadcasting a story deduced from a police or fire transmission. An exception is the report of a traffic accident. You can speak of a reported traffic accident at a particular locality, warning people to avoid the area if possible (and perhaps to watch out for emergency vehicles). Even if the report is incorrect, there is sure to be an emergency vehicle speeding to the scene to check it out. Many radio stations, even in large markets, rely on such scanner information for most of their traffic reports.

Fire frequencies are especially helpful in catching traffic accidents because "attention tones" often precede dispatches. In addition, fire and rescue equipment is usually sent routinely to every traffic accident until it's established whether any injuries are involved. Be aware, though, that a great many of the dispatches to fires are false alarms. On fire calls, it's best to wait until the engines arrive and see if there really is a fire before going on the air with the story, unless the fire engines themselves are a traffic hazard.

The modern scanning receiver tunes rapidly across many frequencies, and the frequencies monitored can be entered on a keypad. All that remains is to find out the frequencies that the local agencies use. In my experience, most police and fire agencies are willing to give newspeople these frequencies, and they generally assume that the media are monitoring their transmissions.

Any frequencies you can't obtain in this manner can sometimes be found by using a "seeking" feature, which many modern scanning receivers offer. You enter a starting frequency and an ending frequency, and the receiver automatically scans every possible frequency between them in a methodical manner, stopping on active channels and letting you save them if you wish. This can be particularly helpful in obtaining confidential frequencies, such as those used by the FBI and other government agencies.

Some police and fire agencies are moving toward computer dispatching; if only this sort of telemetry is available in your area, you may have to find a way to receive the computer data. I understand that most of the departments using this system not only have kept a radio system active after the terminals were installed in the cars, but also have offered the news media a chance to "subscribe" to their computer system. This subscription is probably worth the cost if it's the only way to monitor emergency communications.

Staying on top of local emergencies gives your station a chance to be ahead of the local newspapers—and usually ahead of television stations—on the "curiosity factor" news. Being first with such news is a way to establish with listeners what station they can depend on when they "need to know."

A couple of hints to get the most from a scanning receiver: Always have the "scan delay" option switched on; this prevents the receiver from scanning onward immediately after a provocative or interesting communication, allowing you a chance to catch the other half of the conversation and to identify the channel and its source. Post a list of the frequencies and agencies, keyed to the "channel number" on your scanner, so that interesting or cryptic exchanges can be followed by a telephone call to the agency from which it originated. If you don't know which channel the communication was on, you may have a frustrating time tracking down the source for the story.

One way of pursuing the legitimate news events you learn about via your newsroom scanner—a bad accident, a major robbery, a fire— is to call the person or location involved or one nearby. Don't overlook people who live on the same block and can look out a window and describe a breaking situation for you by phone as an eyewitness. If you are fortunate enough to be located in a city large enough to have a published reverse phone directory, spend the money and buy it. In these directories, addresses are listed sequentially by street and number. You can look up the address given on the scanner, or one nearby, and then call the number shown for that location to try to get an interview.

I believe that the telephone is still radio's most important news-gathering tool. You should have tape (or its equivalent) rolling on all of your news calls. Unfortunately, because of deejays' hoaxing people on the air in "funny" phone calls, the FCC has tightened its rules about putting phone calls on the air. This has given reporters an unnecessary handicap.

Before the FCC crackdown in the early eighties, newspeople routinely taped all calls and asked permission only at the end of the call to use the taped material on the air. By then, the interviewee had finished talking, was satisfied with what he or she said, and almost always agreed. Today, you must advise subjects that you're recording them *before* starting the interview. This sometimes makes them nervous and they refuse, or else they become reticent and you get nothing usable.

When this is likely to be a problem, a strategy some newspeople use is greeting the person they are calling as follows: "Hello, this is XXX of WXXX radio news tape is rolling and I wonder if I could ask you a question or two about . . ." By speeding past the recording advisory (which is worded a bit too obscurely for the average person to notice anyway), it is possible to give legal notification without the other party being fully aware of it.

This potentially risky approach ethically *requires* that you end the call with a formal request for permission to broadcast parts of the interview and that you not use the tape if the subject says no. If you choose this tactic, in case the subject later complains to the FCC, charging that you didn't give the advisory at the *start* of the call as required (a rule enforced by large fines), you had better save the tape for a significant period of time to serve in your defense. Of course, if you don't get permission to use the tape on the air, you can still write a story making use of the key material obtained in the interview. (Record a voicer!)

Following are a few more unorthodox but potentially very productive ways and places to find news material.

Shortwave Radio

Although I feel strongly that radio stations should concentrate their news coverage on local and regional stories, this does not mean that major national and international stories should be ignored. The wire services routinely cover these stories, as do the networks. However, my own preference is not to air the network reports but to read the important national and international stories, in brief, near the end of the locally oriented newscast.

However, when there is a major international story, you may be able to cover it yourself faster and better than the wire services and networks by using a high-quality, digitally tuned shortwave radio that is wired into the news console for recording. Make sure that it has a good antenna system and that you have nearby a shortwave reference, such as Billboard Publications' annual *World Radio TV Handbook*, which lists frequencies and transmission times for the world's shortwave broadcasters. (This book is sold at ham radio supply stores, among other places.)

It is generally permissible for U.S. newspeople to tape and rebroadcast international shortwave radio transmissions without obtaining prior permission, but this definitely does *not* apply to broadcasts that originate within the United States, such as the "Voice of America." You may find that the news audio you get in this way may be as much as half a day ahead of similar information on the wire services; that's what I found when I taped and rebroadcast BBC summaries on the Falklands War between England and Argentina in the early eighties.

Amateur Radio Operators

Amateur radio enthusiasts, or hams, exchange information with others all over the world. Through the nearest electronics store catering to hams, you should be able to find a radio amateur willing to serve as a news source for you when disaster strikes around the world. When an earthquake or similar catastrophe occurs, the first communication with the outside world usually occurs through ham radio operators. Although it is not legal to rebroadcast radio traffic from the ham bands (or CB bands), a cooperative amateur radio enthusiast can notify you when he or she picks up radio traffic from a disaster scene and can summarize for you (on tape, for sound bites) the latest information. On more than one occasion, my stations have been first in the country with details of a disaster story through this simple means.

Experts

You can customize and localize a national or international story by contacting experts on the subject or country involved at a nearby college or university. These can be a great resource for you. These people can frequently provide a depth of background to clarify and explain complex international events, and their very presence on your air provides a local angle to the story. In addition, they may be aware of other local angles, such as local residents with close associations to the region or the people around which the story centers, who you can contact for additional interviews. Although your use of local authorities to enrich a distant story will be copied by other media, listeners do notice who leads in innovative news coverage (and so do those local experts)!

Inside Sources

You certainly don't have to rely entirely on outside sources to come up with stories. Odd little things you notice while driving around town often have an interesting and undiscovered story behind them. If something that you come across surprises or puzzles you, look into it.

Don't overlook one additional source for news items: your own staff! Encourage your airstaff, salespeople, and secretaries to call in with reports on traffic jams, fires, and interesting or puzzling things that they come across. They will be happy to do it if you encourage them. You get news leads, and it makes your staff feel more a part of the station's on-air product. Don't greet any items coming from these people with "Oh, we already knew about that" or "That's not really news." One comment like this and they'll never call in again. Thank them at the very least, and use the information if you can. Occasionally, it'll really be important.

The Strategic Advantage of a Small News Staff

The approaches listed above do not require a large staff. In fact, I recommend that you maintain as small a staff as possible to keep from falling into the laziness of routine that large radio news departments, which feel comfortably staffed, often seem to experience. Even just one strongly motivated newsperson—someone who gets an adrenaline rush from scooping the competing media day after day—is worth ten unmotivated reporters.

Furthermore, a small news department can become far more productive if the newspeople do not have to sit in the station preparing and delivering the newscasts. This thought seems incomprehensible to most of the radio people I've discussed it with; they seem to think that the very purpose of newspeople is to deliver the news. They think that a station sounds bigger when "another voice" does news. Once again, here's something that radio people believe—but listeners don't.

All that the listeners really want from newscasts are the facts from a dependable source. It doesn't matter if the deejays read the news; it's what they report that's important. Hire your newspeople for their ability to root out the news stories. You may even be able to hire a top-notch newspaper reporter with a poor voice if he or she seldom goes on the air.

If you find the right motivated newspeople, try this: Limit their required time in the station to the period before 9 A.M. or some other short interval. Instead of requiring them to read newscasts on the air, have them gather and prepare news stories—putting an emphasis on sound bites when possible—and have the deejays deliver the news. Then, give the newspeople the rest of the day to use at their discretion. Set goals for the number of meaningful stories they produce, not the hours they spend in a chair in the newsroom.

Promoting Your Station as a News Source

Once your news approach is focused and vitalized, promote it by making recorded "promos" from the best on-scene reports or the most dramatic first-person actualities or sound bites. Run each new promo hourly for a couple of days, calling attention to the work of your news department. Some program directors have a standard prerecorded open and close standing by for such promos so that all that's necessary is to drop in the audio while dubbing to tape cartridge (or equivalent), and it's done immediately. (If it's not easy to make these promos, they won't get done.)

Despite the co-op nature of wire services like AP, some stations discourage the staff from sharing their stories with the wire service. This seems very shortsighted to me. Not only is there a psychological (and occasionally financial) reward for newspeople in simply seeing their name and call letters on a wire story, but it's a good way for news personnel to build a reputation—and the station's reputation at the same time—as a news source. In addition, it puts psychological pressure on the other stations with which you compete. It's a little intimidating for them to see your station credited with stories, particularly if it happens time and again.

But the most important reason for giving your stories to a wire service or network after you've used them is that it validates your journalism. If you have stories no other source reports, your listeners may conclude that the stories weren't as important as your station thought. They might even wonder if you made them up or got them all wrong. On the other hand, if a pattern develops of your station reporting stories first, followed by other stations and media reporting them later, you not only slowly emerge as the news leader in listeners' minds, but the importance of the stories you report is *enhanced* by their appearance later on other stations and in the newspapers.

Another technique for promoting the station's news and the station itself (while intimidating the competition) is winning news awards. There are a number of news competitions in which you can enter your station, and—let me make this clear—to win the news award you *must* enter the competition. These awards aren't somehow just bestowed on stations deemed deserving. You'll never win a news award if you don't enter news contests. If you do enter, your chances of winning are usually better than you think because most stations don't enter.

You can find a listing of the major news awards in each year's *Broadcasting and Cable Yearbook*. Also, check with your state broadcasters' association (you'll find the address and phone number in the *Yearbook*) and your wire service. Both often offer regional news awards.

You aren't likely to win a news award if you don't have *audio* of the story or coverage that you're submitting. Get your newspeople thinking about saving their best actualities and on-scene voicers, and make sure that your staff routinely runs airchecks of ongoing coverage of breaking news stories or disaster coverage. Buy lots of decent-quality tape cassettes, and save everything that might possibly constitute an entry. The best stuff may not strike you as "award quality" until you look back on it later.

Public Affairs Programming

In addition to its requirement for news coverage, the FCC used to require a certain amount of public affairs programming. Once it abolished that requirement, many stations stopped bothering with public affairs programming. That's very shortsighted because the FCC still mandates that each station present some programming every week to address local community problems. (You'll find more about this in Chapter 12.) This bit of governmental deregulation actually means that you can now devote your public affairs effort to worthwhile activities without worrying too much about the number of minutes you devote to it.

The term *public affairs* refers to a discussion of the issues outside of a newscast. (The FCC does not recognize news programming as meeting the requirement to address community problems and issues.) Any public affairs programming you offer should be detailed for the Public Inspection File that the FCC requires every station to maintain. I'll go into detail on how to do this in Chapter 12, but in essence, you must document how you addressed the community problems that the station has identified as significant.

The management of the station (which often means you, the program director) must prepare a list of these community problems, using his or her best judgment, and put it in the station's Public Inspection File on the first of January, April, July, and October of each year. (Make sure that somebody is doing this at your station. There are big fines for stations that fail to do so.) This list of community problems, often ranked number 1 through 10 in importance, should also be given to the news staff every three months. Encourage your newspeople to address these programs in public affairs programming; the FCC expects the station to run programs discussing those issues.

When you prepare a regular public affairs program—these often appear on Sunday mornings—you might consider promoting listenership by lifting sound bites from these upcoming shows for use in prior newscasts when an interesting and newsworthy point is made in the interview. Be sure to tag the story with the comment that the complete interview is to be presented, and say when.

You can go even farther in your thinking. How can you involve the station in a community issue (and not just as a benefactor or donator of time and talent, as most stations do)? How about doing a remote deejay show from the scene of some controversial local activity or event? "Remotes" are usually used in radio just as a sales vehicle. Yet by placing the station's broadcasts right in the middle of a major event in the community—a controversial agricultural spraying program, a legislative or civic crisis, a weather emergency—and doing the station's regular shows from this location while incorporating ongoing reporting of the event, you gain visibility that participating in parades can never give you. This can be powerful and documentable public affairs programming—and award-entry material, too.

Here's an example of what I mean: When I was programming KEX radio in Portland, Oregon, in the seventies, one of my on-air personalities, Nick Diamond, came up with an idea that made for great radio and great public affairs programming. He did his Saturday night deejay show live, using the station's high-fidelity two-way radio system, from the backseat of an on-duty Portland police car.

By incorporating the routine (but often exciting) police assignments on which the police car was sent, while announcing the records being played at the studio and reading live commercials, he succeeded in catching the pulse of the city, showing the police in action in a way that most listeners hadn't yet experienced. He also offered insights into the crime and youth problems of the city. The resulting program was responsive to two of the key concerns of the community as listed at the time: crime and youth. It amounted to a four-hour public affairs program, and it was compelling radio! By the way, I taped the show and submitted it in a national competition, and it won the station a major award.

Use your imagination. If your station has a "Marti"-type portable broadcast-quality transmitter for use in remote broadcasts, make sure that the news department has access to it for projects like this.

News is, by definition, the reporting of events of immediate interest to listeners, and most people are most interested in news that hits close to home. I hope I have convinced you that an aggressive, locally oriented news policy is one of the most potent ways of making your station important to your listeners, no matter what the overall format of the station, and no matter how large or small your market. Because 80 percent or more of all radio listening is to music, I most definitely include music radio stations in this statement. Make it clear to your listeners what your station's news "mission" is, and then deliver on that promise.

When News Is All the Station Offers

What, then, of All-News formats? The same sort of aggressive, locally oriented news policy will pay off handsomely for such stations because listeners are already prepared to believe that a station specializing in news will do the best job of covering it. However, listeners also have the most uncompromising expectations of stations making such a promise. If your station falls short of meeting their expectations, they will be open to a less-encompassing but dependable news promise made by stations for which news is just one ingredient. This has been the focus of much of this chapter up until now.

The main difficulty in bringing to life an aggressive, locally oriented All-News radio station is the enormous expense that is usually involved. To do the best locally oriented news job at all hours and every day of the week is usually considered impossibly costly; thus All-News stations usually make extensive use of network material, which by its nature is not local. This opens the door for news competition from all of the other radio stations in the market. It leaves the All-News station making no promise other than that some sort of news will always be on, whenever people choose to listen. This promise often isn't kept either, particularly on the so-called News-Talk stations, which rely on syndicated telephone talk programs during nonpeak hours.

It has always struck me that if there is a radio format that most lends itself to automation, it is probably an aggressive, locally oriented All-News operation. The most rudimentary of automation systems would work—even just chains of sequentially triggered tape cartridge machines. The automation would be used simply for delivery of the news, freeing the news staff for gathering and recording stories and summaries. Yet, as far as I know, there has never been an All-News station in any market that has made thorough use of this concept.

Ironically, the modern radio newsroom is frequently highly automated in newswriting, copy retrieval, news wire delivery, and even sound-bite storage, editing, and playback but maintains a substantial, costly studio staff to manage the whole thing in real time. The idea I offer is that a really good news staff of very small size—essentially no larger than an average station deejay staff—be assembled to gather news, package news on tape cartridge or similar audio system, read complementary wire copy in recorded continuity summaries, cart up any network material felt to be complementary, and set up a playback sequence emphasizing the most important (usually local or regional) stories. Prerecorded formatting materials would be inserted frequently to provide the sense of station identity and establish listener expectations.

Most of the time, no more than one person would be needed on duty at the studio of such a station to do telephone interviews, record tape cartridges or the equivalent, keep up with the news wire, and baby-sit the playback system. Any other on-duty personnel would be in the field gathering news and audio as needed. Such remote reporting would be telephoned or radioed back to the station—perhaps directly into the automation system, complete with coding for how it should be handled in the sequence, if the automation system is sufficiently sophisticated and computerized for that. I don't see why such an operation need cost significantly more than a similar-sized music station to run, making All-News an aggressive, profitable option even in small markets.

If this concept doesn't interest you, perhaps it has stimulated some original ideas about using technology to improve the service that your station offers its listeners—without losing the human element that provides the main reason for listener attention and loyalty.

The thought I'd like to leave with you as this chapter ends is that news can be a potent programming weapon for stations in any format but that what is presented in the newscast has to be relevant—and hopefully compelling—to the listener in order to realize its potential. Furthermore, this vital newscast must be packaged to emphasize what it is that makes it unique and to establish proper listener expectations—expectations that must then be consistently fulfilled if they are to build and maintain the station's aggressive news image.

What is the general public's key expectation of radio news, which most stations so consistently fail to live up to and which few radio people even strive for? Immediacy, reliability, and always being first with the important stories as they break. If you establish and then consistently meet this expectation, you'll own a potent news image that no overstaffed competitor will ever be able to overcome.

7

Promoting Your Station

The Purposes of Promotion

Promotion of a radio station can be described as having, essentially, three possible purposes: (1) to recycle or extend the listening of the station's audience, thus building the station's audience share; (2) to attract new listeners, thus building the station's cumulative ratings; or (3) to establish and enhance the station's image and listener expectations without a specific immediate rating goal. (If a specific audience-building goal is set for a promotion, one of the first two types of promotional efforts will be required to achieve that goal.)

Every promotional idea must be evaluated within the context of these three objectives and should be implemented only if it advances one or more of these purposes. Furthermore, it should be specifically shaped to home in most directly on the primary goal. This thought might seem obvious, but even at the largest stations, most promotional ideas arise from opportunity or economic (usually sponsor-oriented) concerns.

Economics are essential for station survival, but the goal of all station promotions must be listener-oriented and consistent with the station's image and format if they are to have a positive effect on the station and its future. The revenue-raising goals of the station must be incorporated into a promotion after it is designed with these thoughts in mind. Economic concerns must not compromise any element of the station's image and goals.

95

This is the point in the book where a cry of anguish arising from deep in the soul of your sales manager or general manager may interrupt your reading. If so, let me assure them of my empathy. I have been a successful radio salesperson and a general manager, so it is not only from my background in programming assignments that I make that emphatic point; I do it from all three of those perspectives.

Your station's audio product must shape and then meet the clear expectations of your audience or you will have no one to sell to. Stations that dismiss the idea that programming comes before sales as foolish nonsense or unworldly impracticality will eventually lose all of their audience. The audio *product* that the station is in business to provide must come first—always.

With that point made, do understand that program and promotion people can frequently be inspired by economic needs to produce a strong, listener-oriented promotional idea with which a sponsor can be accommodated. The economic need may indeed be served, but the resulting promotion must be listener-oriented and dictated by the image and needs of the station and its product.

On-Air Contests

Probably the best-remembered, most spectacular contest in radio history—the copyrighted creation of Jack McCoy's Ram Research Company—was the Last Contest, which was first used in San Diego. It was inspired from the beginning by economic goals and the desire to sell participation to a variety of sponsors. Nonetheless, the packaging and design fully met the standards I've just laid out for radio promotion. Usually, a promotion should have a single focus: either promotion to the station's own listeners or promotion to attract potential new listeners. The Last Contest had a dual focus, although it was more oriented to the station's own audience than to nonlisteners. This promotion is worth studying.

The Last Contest was conducted on the air, offering many dozen well-constructed prize packages filled with compatible, "dream prize" elements. Each was described ("romanced") on the air and identified by prize package number. For example, a prize package might be described as follows: "A brand-new house, with all the furnishings, landscaping service and maintenance for five years for the acre of land it sits on, and with matching cars for every member of the family to fill the big garage. In addition, we'll include a ten-year credit at a supermarket for all the food to feed your family . . . and several hundred of your friends."

It sounded like the station had spent millions of dollars on the prizes. In fact, though, sponsors had paid the station for the privilege of offering the prizes and participating in the contest. The sponsors were required to provide the prizes they were offering *only* if the winning listener chose their prize package from among the many offered. In this case, the extra publicity involving the winner would compensate for the additional expense.

There was just one winner, determined by random selection of a telephone caller at a special phone number. The telephone number was disclosed on the air only at the moment when the contest was to climax with a winner; the randomly selected winner then chose one of the prize packages. That certainly encouraged sustained listening over a considerable period of time; however, there was nothing in the promotion to build long-term or repeat listening to the station once the contest had ended.

This contest blew out phone exchanges at its climax, strongly enhanced the ratings of the station it appeared on while the contest was in progress, and made a great deal of money for the station, too. A warning: As far as I know, the copyright on this concept is still being enforced, and you are still subject to prosecution if you copy it too closely. I describe it here simply to stimulate your own thinking.

A blockbuster promotion like the Last Contest can be promoted outside the station and can attract new audience. In general, however, new listeners who tune in specifically to try to win a contest don't continue to listen after the contest is over. For on-air promotions, I suggest that your imagination move in the direction of promotions that do enhance the long-term listening expectations of the audience so that any ratings gains are more than temporary.

On-air contests for your listeners can be designed to encourage extended listening, but I've noticed that the fun goes out of them for many listeners if it's too obvious that you're trying to manipulate them and their listening patterns. Extended listening can be encouraged in an entertaining way with contests in which listeners accumulate clues to help win a prize, but the most important factors in radio contests are listener participation and immediate response, and those factors are introduced by the use of the phone.

Contests involving the listener mailing in an entry have no immediacy and don't draw a fraction of the response that a phone contest does. Telephone contests involve some element of chance—guessing something or selecting a choice—and using rotating cuts on a tape cartridge enforces random selection.

In contests in which listeners might be motivated to try to figure out the sequence of cuts on a cartridge, two identically labeled carts should be used, with the cut sequence of one done in reverse on the other. To ensure that the cuts won't occur twice in the same order on the air, the cartridge to be used each time the contest is played should be selected at random by the on-air person.

The most important function of such contests is "formatting fun." Because most listeners never call in to participate, the contest should be devised to be fun to listen to and should be broadcast frequently enough to become an important continuing element of the programming. Playing such a contest once an hour works well as long as the point in the hour in which the contest is played doesn't become predictable.

By the way, it's very important to have the listener's voice on the air during the contest. Some stations worry about the possible hazards of the listener appearing live on the air, but I've found that radio's standard seven-second delay is rarely necessary in this particular case. Unless you have cause to believe that your listeners are different—in which case you'll have to take precautions—my experience is that if listeners are put on the air only to make a guess or a choice, they never throw away their chance to win by using that opportunity to say something offensive.

The prize offered should be nice enough to warrant the listener's effort to call in and play and to keep the station from sounding cheap, but a large or spectacular prize is unnecessary. In fact, it can actually reduce listener interest and participation by seeming unattainable. Cash always makes a desirable prize, and it doesn't have to be a lot to attract interest, particularly if the contest itself is fun to listen to and play.

You must figure out the odds of winning and design the contest accordingly to stay within the budget and complete the scheduled run on the air. It should go without saying that you must never "manage" the contest after it's designed! You must never alter the odds or control in any way when a win will occur or who may win. Any such tampering is fraud, and the Federal Communications Commission can and has levied large fines and even revoked station licenses because of it, even if no actual harm resulted.

Take pains to keep your contests fair and honest. I suggest opening a special "contests" section in your Public Inspection File and putting all contest materials, rules and scripts, and "player sheets" in it. Then you will have evidence of fairness if a disappointed or malicious listener later chooses to raise charges of rigging.

The "Astrology" Game

It may be useful to present here an example of the type of on-air telephone contest I'm talking about. This example will show how a contest should be scripted to make sure that the key elements of the rules are given consistently and that all contestants have an equal chance to win. The following is one of my favorites. It's fun for the contestant, it's fun for the deejay, and it's fun for listeners, even if they never actively participate. This one also demonstrates how a small budget and some knowledge of the mathematics of odds can make a modest contest budget sound rather substantial, both legitimately and fairly.

This is a birthday game. I usually refer to it as an astrology game, even though it has nothing to do with astrology or birth signs, because the name lends itself to production and conveys an element of the mysterious. Unlike most rotating-cut cartridge games, listeners in this case do not have to guess something that must match what's next on the cart. In this example, they are simply intent on seeing if the month they were born in has "already been selected." ("Whether you're about to win was determined years ago on the very day you were born!")

Staying within Budget and Calculating Odds

Before I get to sample scripts, let's first go through the budgeting for the contest and the figuring of odds. Let's set up some guidelines.

We'll want to play this contest often—once an hour between 6 A.M. and midnight, seven days a week. That's 126 times a week (18 times a day × 7 days per week), and we'd like to play it for four weeks.

That's a total of 504 games (126 games × 4 weeks). Because listeners will try to match the month of their birth, there are twelve possible choices. With all twelve months appearing an equal number of times on our rotating tape cartridges (but in varying random orders), the odds are that we'll have a one-in-twelve chance of getting a winner each time we play the game. That's the same as having one winner every twelve games. Thus when the game is played 504 times, we need only to divide 12 into that number to come up with the approximate number of winners we will have: forty-two.

Suppose, now, that we want to offer at least a $20 prize for each win, but 42 times $20 is $840, and we have only a $500 contest budget for the whole month. One solution is to reduce the number of contests to bring the winners down to budget level. Divide $20 per winner into $500, and that's 25 winners. Because the odds of winning are one in twelve, multiply 25 by 12 to find the number of contests needed to generate twenty-five winners: That's three hundred contests.

Divide 126 contests per week into 300 contests, and it looks as though we can stay within budget by limiting the contest to 2.38 weeks, or two weeks and a little over two days. That's not long enough, however! A contest like this is only just becoming widely known to your listeners after two and a third weeks, and it really should run a whole month for maximum impact. You must give the listeners a chance to get really well acquainted with it before it ends.

Another solution to this budget problem is to reduce the number of contests per day. Assume four weeks and three hundred contests. Divide 300 by 4, and that's seventy-five contests per week. Divide 75 by 7, and that's 10.7 contests per day—say, ten a day. That means that if we want to play the game between 6 A.M. and midnight, we're going to have to skip the contest in 8 of these 18 hours every day, preferably skipping different hours each day. I find that this sort of limitation really does damage the momentum of a contest like this; it should be played once an hour.

Maybe we could reduce the contest to a three-week promotion? Three hundred divided by 3 is one hundred chances per week; 100 divided by 7 days per week is 14.28, or fourteen contests a day. We only have to skip four of the eighteen hours each day in order to run the contest for three weeks between 6 A.M. and midnight, or we could limit it to running between 6 A.M. and 8 P.M. That's better, though not ideal.

Here's the best solution. It not only allows the contest to run as planned—once per hour, 18 hours a day, for 4 weeks—but it permits a bigger prize to be offered within the $500 budget and adds a provocative choice to the contest that the players and the listeners will both enjoy. We'll simply add a second level to the contest. Once contestants have "matched" their birth month to the randomly selected cut on the cartridge and have won $20, they'll be offered an intriguing choice: Will they risk that $20 to win, say, a $200 prize by trying to match the numerical day of the month they were born? Most listeners are likely to regard $20 "in the hand" as worth more than $200 "in the bush," and if they have to give up the whole $20 to take a chance at a second win, most won't do it. Suppose, though, that they still get $5 if they gamble on the second level and lose?

In my experience, most contestants will take that gamble because they still get some of their original cash winnings if they lose. The nonplaying listeners will make a choice, mentally, with the contestants—and then will listen to see if they would have won if they had taken the chance on the second level.

Notice what has happened here: With eighteen contests per day, seven days a week for four weeks, we understood that we'd play 504 contests and have forty-two winners. If 90 percent of those winners (nine of every ten winners) go on to level 2 and try to match the numerical date of the month they were born (on which the odds are only 1 in 31), only four or five winners in the entire four weeks will take the $20, and the rest will receive $5 if they don't win the second level.

If, over four weeks, five listeners take the $20 they won in the first level and stop, that uses up $100 of our $500 budget. That leaves thirty-seven first-level winners who will receive the $5 consolation prize, accounting for another $185 of our $500 budget. This means that we're spending approximately $285 on those first-level winners, leaving $215 for the big prize in the second level of the contest—for which we plan a $200 prize. (We have $15 left in the budget if an extra contestant chooses to stop and keep the $20 won at the first level.)

What about that $200 prize? What are the odds that someone will win that prize? We're planning 504 contests. The odds of the big win—in which a contestant matches their birth month (1 in 12) and then their birth date in the month (1 in 31) is equal to 12 months times 31 days, or 1 in 372. We get 1.35 when we divide 504 contests by 372, so there should be one and a third $200 winners. In other words, we should have one $200 winner for sure, but there's only a 33 percent chance of a second one. That's 2-to-1 odds against having a second $200 winner.

If the general manager will agree to raise your budget to $700 if a second big winner does beat the odds during the four weeks of the contest, you're covered. Even though this two-level structure reduces the cash payout for the contest compared to the single-level game, you are now able to tell listeners honestly and fairly that "you can win up to $200 cash every time we play the game." The contest sounds more exciting, the basic prize still sounds winnable, and the extra choice for the contestant makes the game more fun to play and hear.

You'll notice I mention tape cartridges exclusively in discussing the playing of these "random selection" carted contests. There is a good chance at your station you will have put the old cart machines in the back room and are now using digital audio storage. For this type of contest, I urge you to resurrect the cart machines for this purpose only! The reason is that tape cartridges have a very important advantage in conducting this sort of contest: The random order of the cuts on the cart are as much a mystery to your airstaff as it is to your listeners. Since carts cannot be previewed and then rewound back one cut—the tape can only move in one direction—you have the means of proving randomness to listeners if it's in question, and you prevent any possibility that one of your airstaff could "rig" the contest in favor of a particular player. Digital media do not have this sort of safeguard. Keep a couple of functioning cart machines handy specifically for contests like this!

In keeping with my earlier comments about how to record contest cartridges: If you do this contest, you should have either twenty-four or thirty-six cuts on each of the two "month" carts, with either two or three (respectively) repeats of each month, in a different random sequence of twelve each time, with whatever sequence of months you worked out for the first cart done in reverse order on the second cart. Use two physically identical carts—identically labeled, so that the deejays can't tell them apart. The sequence of winning months on the carts thus can't be figured out by either your listeners or your airstaff, so the odds you've calculated should apply and the contest will be fair.

However, because the second level of the contest, involving a "numerical date" cart, will be played at least twelve times less often than the first level, it seems sufficient to work out a random sequence in which the calendar dates 1 to 31 are included once—with the same thirty-one numbers occurring after the first in a different sequence— for a total of sixty-two cuts on a single cart. That sequence won't complete itself even once during the whole run of the contest because the odds indicate only a maximum of forty-two opportunities to use it, so there's no need for a second tape cartridge for this level of the contest.

In this example, we now know how often we'll play the game, what the prize will be, and that it will be a two-level challenge. Listeners won't have to guess anything in making the selection at either level of the contest but will simply reveal a fact about their birth date. Thus our promos can point out that "if you were born, you can win" or "whether you win the Astrology Game was determined on the day you were born" and so forth.

Again, the contest is a lot of fun not only for the contestants and the airstaff, but also for the majority of your listeners who will never call in but who will hear it a number of times during the month. Every time they hear the game played, they'll listen to see if their month is the winner that time. If the contestant wins the first level, they'll second-guess whether they would have gone on to the second level, and—if so—they will wait to see if their own birth date would have won.

Now that you've used a calculator to work out the odds and to reconcile the prize and the number of contests with the budget, it's time to schedule the contest with the traffic department, write the scripts, and then write a memo to the staff describing the contest and how they're to run it. You should tell them all this verbally, too, but having it in writing (put a copy in the Public Inspection File) is legal protection for everyone involved.

Writing the Scripts

As I mentioned earlier, the scripts are designed to cover all of the important points every time the contest is played and to ensure that each contestant has an equal opportunity to win. Any ad-libbing per-

Astrology Contest Script 1

Start contest going into last record before the break:

"JUST HAVING BEEN BORN IS ALL IT TAKES TO PLAY AND WIN WXXX's ASTROLOGY GAME! IF YOU'D LIKE TO LET YOUR BIRTHDAY PAY OFF FOR YOU IN CASH, CALL ME RIGHT NOW. I'LL TAKE CALL NUMBER XX."

Going into spot break, after caller is selected:

"THIS HOUR, OUR XXth CALLER IN THE WXXX ASTROLOGY CONTEST WAS <name> OF <city>. WE'LL PLAY THE GAME FOR WXXX CASH IN JUST A MINUTE!"

Play contest last in break, before jingle and record:

"THE CONTESTANT THIS HOUR IN OUR WXXX ASTROLOGY GAME IS <name> OF <city>, WHO WILL TRY TO MATCH UP <his/her> MONTH OF BIRTH WITH THE MONTH WE'VE PRESELECTED AT RANDOM. IF IT MATCHES, THE CASH PRIZE IS TWENTY DOLLARS! <first name>, IF YOU'RE READY, TELL US THE MONTH YOU WERE BORN!"
 <Pot up/log month on form/have them repeat>
"ALL RIGHT, LET'S SEE NOW IF THAT MONTH MATCHES!"
<Play the cart>
<Pot up for reaction>

If contestant loses:

"I'M SORRY, YOU WEREN'T A WINNER THIS TIME, BUT YOU CAN PLAY AGAIN AS EARLY AS TOMORROW. THANKS FOR LISTENING TO WXXX!"
If contestant wins, see Script 2.

Astrology Contest Script 2

Second level—after contestant matches month of birth:

"CONGRATULATIONS! YOU'VE JUST WON TWENTY DOLLARS IN CASH FROM WXXX!"
<Pot up for reaction>
"NOW, YOU HAVE A CHOICE: YOU CAN STOP NOW AND KEEP THE TWENTY DOLLARS, OR YOU CAN GO ON AND TRY TO MATCH THE DATE OF THE MONTH YOU WERE BORN FOR *TWO HUNDRED DOL-LARS!* IF YOU TRY FOR THE BIG CASH PRIZE AND MISS, YOU'LL STILL GET FIVE DOLLARS FROM WXXX, SO RIGHT NOW YOU'RE A CASH WINNER EITHER WAY! NOW, <name>, ARE YOU GOING TO GO FOR THE TWO HUNDRED DOLLARS CASH PRIZE OR NOT?"
<Pot up for response>

If contestant refuses:

"WELL, JUST BY BEING BORN YOU WON TWENTY DOLLARS FROM WXXX, AND WE'LL MAIL YOU THE CHECK SHORTLY."
<Pot up for reaction>
"THANKS FOR LISTENING TO WXXX!" <jingle/record>

If contestant agrees:

"GOOD FOR YOU! NOW, TELL US THE NUMERICAL DATE OF THE DAY YOU WERE BORN, AND IF IT MATCHES THE DATE BETWEEN 1 AND 31 WE'VE ALREADY PRESELECTED AT RANDOM, YOU WIN TWO HUNDRED DOLLARS! NOW, <first name>, WHAT'S THAT DATE??"
<Pot up for response/log it on form/have then repeat/play cart>

If contestant loses:

"TOO BAD—BUT YOU'RE STILL A CASH WINNER, AND YOU'LL GET A CHECK FOR FIVE DOLLARS FROM WXXX! THANKS FOR PLAYING THE GAME!"
If contestant wins, congratulate him or her and milk it! The contestant has won $200!!!

Table 7.1

Astrology Contest Player Sheet

Date and Day:_____

Name	Address	City/Zip	Phone	Month	Date	$ Won?

<Return sheet to program director at end of day>

mitted the air talent during the game must include all elements of the script in the order in which they are presented. A script also helps make sure that the contest is run in tight and purposeful fashion.

The samples that follow show how the script might be written. A sample player sheet—on which each contestant's name and address is recorded with his or her birth month and date and the prize won—is presented in Table 7.1.

These scripts and forms are strictly samples. You'll want to tailor your scripts and player sheets to the requirements of your station and to the individual contest. The forms presented should give you an idea of what you'll need.

What Promotions Must Accomplish

Probably the most important point made in this chapter is that all promotions—whether contests, participation in civic events, or what have you—must be done only when the station management clearly understands what it expects to achieve with them. Then promotions must be planned and executed to attain the station's goals.

This is obvious, yet radio station promotions, especially those done off the air, are seldom held to that standard. It's very tempting to be a "good citizen" and do whatever community leaders request (participating in community events they're promoting and so forth), but most station participation in civic events achieves nothing measurable for the station.

How will sponsoring a charity footrace gain the station even one listener? The station's call letters will be on posters and maybe on T-shirts, but since when do people feel obligated to listen, or even become interested in listening, to stations listed on posters? When do they change their listening patterns to check out stations on T-shirts?

It may seem crass, but it really isn't. The station deserves to benefit as much as do the events or organizations it is asked to support. As the program director, you will usually be the primary person responsible for seeing to it that the station does benefit. This calls for imagination and an understanding of your audience.

If the station wants to put on its own civic fund-raiser, devise an event that will clearly be the station's own rather than an event the station will simply participate in. For example, suppose you are planning a chili cook-off. Consider how a sales promotion can be built into the event, such as selling sponsorships in which advertisers give "free discount vouchers" to reduce the cost of the tickets sold at the door. (Former KMPC, Los Angeles, program director Mark Blinoff devised such a successful annual promotion.)

Although sponsor-originated or sales-oriented promotions all too often prostitute the station and its image to make a quick buck, when a promotion is shaped to meet the goals of the station, sponsors can and should profitably be involved in it. In addition, if the promotion will be conducted on the air—and most are—let me strongly urge that the station only have one promotion going at a time. Although it may seem logical that if one promotion is good, several at once would be even more exciting, that doesn't relate to the pattern-oriented, somewhat preoccupied way that audiences listen to the radio.

After all, radio is the soundtrack of people's lives; it provides the audio background while their attention is directed somewhere else. Thus, although one major, well-conceived promotion can be a plus for listeners, two or more concurrent promotions just blur any positive perception or expectation. The station just seems busy, confusing, and cluttered.

Radio people often completely overlook one source of outside promotion for the station: placing stories in the printed media. Write your story in the form of a press release whenever your station has something potentially newsworthy to report. Even the hiring or promoting of a staff member can be news.

Get to know local newspaper reporters and editors, and call them when something of interest happens in the local media—or involving your own station. Treat them ethically and honestly, and you'll have a good contact. A "news item" about the station seems objective and carries a lot more weight than obvious self-promotion.

I also suggest that you join a local service club. The original (and often still the most influential) is Rotary International. Service clubs put you in contact with local civic leaders and businesspeople. They are not there for self-aggrandizement, but if you are sincerely interested in the community, you'll enjoy meeting club members and you'll make useful acquaintances.

In Rotary, in particular, a premium is put on perfect attendance, and when you can't make your own club's weekly meeting, you are encouraged to "make up" the meeting at another Rotary Club. This widens your circle of acquaintances and, to me, is a major advantage of this club. It's good public relations, and you'll probably enjoy the experience, too, as long as you actively enter into the activities of the club.

Outside Advertising

There are a variety of media available for promoting radio. The most commonly used are television, billboards and bus cards, newspapers, and direct mail, in that order. Like radio, television and billboards and bus cards are "intrusive" media. This means that the advertisement reaches consumers without any conscious effort on their part. Essentially, the entire population available to the medium can be reached by it.

Television, like radio, can tell a story; billboards can only communicate a single, uncomplicated thought—one that must be taken in and registered in a second or two as you pass. Television can sell; billboards (and usually bus cards, too) offer no opportunity to motivate, only to inform or remind (very briefly).

Furthermore, in both television and billboards, placement of the ad is everything. Do not let these media place your ads for you unless you implicitly trust the person handling your account. Given a choice, these media usually place your ads in the remaining positions that all of their other clients didn't choose, and this greatly diminishes the results.

Advertising in newspapers (and sometimes other media) can be available on a reciprocal trade basis, which benefits both parties and makes a decent ad "showing" affordable. If you have a choice, the right-hand side of "page 3" is widely considered to be the best spot in the paper for advertising. However, from a practical point of view, the most effective way to use newspaper advertising is probably to design a relatively small but eye-catching ad and to repeat it at intervals throughout the same issue of the newspaper. Newspapers are not intrusive, and less than 10 percent of the readers ever notice the ads because they look at the paper for its news content. Frequency—repeating the ad—works best on radio and television, and it also works well in catching the reader's attention in print. Yet, hardly any advertisers have caught on to that—particularly since the newspapers feel bound to maintain the fiction that one ad reaches their whole circulation! Your ad is likely to stand out if you use this technique.

Direct-mail advertising is expensive, and a 1 to 2 percent response rate is considered very good in this inefficient medium. Most commonly, radio uses direct mail to promote audience-building contests; this can work, but usually only temporarily. When the promotion is over, the new audience members, who were only tuning in for that contest, stop listening. If you can figure out a direct-mail appeal that calls attention to the station and its service in a manner that will draw interest and response, then you may have a direct-mail piece that will pay off over a long period of time in creating new, lasting audiences.

There is a major problem to overcome once you have selected your medium for promoting the station. It is very hard to communicate what a radio station represents via any of the media described in this section because it's so intangible. We in radio are so close to our medium and our station that it's very hard for us to see how it should be presented visually or in writing to arouse the proper expectations in those who are not already listeners. This results in a great deal of bad and useless advertising.

Earlier in this book I defined *programming* as the art of creating expectations in the minds of listeners and then meeting those expectations whenever they tune in. The goal of most radio station advertising is to arouse appropriate expectations in the minds of nonlisteners and then meet those expectations when they do sample the station. Some outside objectivity is often necessary in pinpointing how to do this effectively, but that's easier said than done.

The problem, and I speak from experience, is that most professional advertising experts don't understand radio. Even big ad agencies generally try to solve this problem by trying to determine what the station executives think the station is and then attempting to depict that. It would be far more useful to spend that effort to determine the image and expectations of the station by its current listeners—and by those who don't listen. Such a study can identify the station's unique appeal for its listeners and, more importantly, discern any misconceptions of the station that may exist in the minds of nonlisteners. This information can then be converted into a striking and effective ad campaign.

Don't spend money on advertising until such research has been done and the resulting strategy and approach has been tested on both listeners and nonlisteners. This precaution may reveal that what seemed so clear to you and your ad agency in fact conveys nothing—or even the wrong message—about the station to those who don't listen to it.

In the meantime, don't overlook the need to keep selling the station to your own listeners. Recorded promos and live "liners" posted on the control board are useful for molding and reinforcing listener perceptions about the station—and even for answering listener questions. When the station wins an award, gets a news scoop, or simply has an interesting bit of station news, get it on the air in a promo of some sort.

When you get a contest winner, for example, have a liner or a carted promo for the event. Have an aircheck tape running routinely when contests are played, to catch each participant's excitement when they win. Don't drop the ball when the winner is determined; most listeners won't have heard the live event and will later be interested in knowing that there was a winner, who it was, what they won, and—if there was something to guess—what the guess was! An audio excerpt of the event itself makes the promo even better.

The goal of promotion and of programming is to create and reinforce listener perceptions. Your work is not done when you've put together a good-sounding on-air product and a fine team of on-air personalities. In fact, your work is only just beginning.

8

Grading Your Programming Performance: What You Need to Know about Ratings

Once upon a time, radio ratings simply estimated the number of listeners age twelve and over ("12+"). In fact, there was a time when they were commonly presented in terms of all listeners age six and over. General circulation newspapers still like to quote radio's audiences in terms of "12+ shares," and you'll usually find them summarized that way in trade magazines, too. Today, though, we are much more concerned with demographics, or specific age groups, and even "psychographics," which refers to lifestyle and attitude.

The reason for this is simple. Ratings are primarily a sales tool, and these days advertisers want to target their advertising to specific groups of people. In fact, the ability to target narrow age groups and lifestyles is one of radio's strengths. Therefore, the ratings for "everybody age 12 and over" are essentially irrelevant today to any radio station's goals, although it's always nice to look good in a ratings display, even that one.

Unfortunately, as radio stations—and advertisers—have become more and more focused in targeting smaller and smaller segments of the population, the ratings become more and more inaccurate. It's not that the research companies are getting sloppier; it's that we are

113

placing more and more burden on their numbers—and the more narrowly we break down individual segments of the ratings, the less confidence we can have on the numbers that result.

Here's why. Radio ratings have been based, since the twenties, on the same technique used in political and opinion polling. Newspapers and magazines are able to develop circulation figures based on what is sent out and what is returned unsold, subtracting the latter from the former and coming up with a hard figure. Of course, this doesn't tell how many of the copies are actually read, which sections are read the most, how many readers there are per copy, and how many of the readers actually read the ads. To obtain this information, the printed media have to resort to the same sort of methodology that radio and television use. Newspapers, in particular, usually want to avoid getting into such unsettling subjects at all because they would be forced to admit that some parts of the paper are read more than other parts. The newspaper ad pricing structure is still based on maintaining the fiction that advertisers achieve similar benefits regardless of where their ads are placed.

Radio and television, however, leave no trail as they depart the transmitter at the speed of light, and there is nothing in the signal to tell how many receivers are tuned to a specific station. Advertisers wanted circulation information, and the opinion-poll technique was pressed into service. The basis of this technique is the law of probability, which in essence states that if you randomly select a small number of people from a given population and determine what they think or do, you can then project the "ratios" (or percentages) of opinion or behavior you find against the whole population within a mathematical percentage of confidence. The larger the sample of the population, the higher the degree of confidence you can have in the results (the smaller the margin of error in the data, in other words).

Of course, if the sample you collect is not a true random cross section of the population, the results become less reliable the less random it is. (However, if it is a random sample of an identifiable subgroup, it can be pretty accurate in representing that subgroup.) We'll spend some time later in this chapter looking at how this problem can cause real trouble in radio ratings results.

The other problem that has developed from using a polling method that was originally limited to yes or no answers, or to selecting a preferred candidate from a very limited number of choices, is that—

as time has gone by—more and more radio stations (choices) are measured in each survey. In even small markets, there may be twenty or more stations listed in the rating book; in large markets, more than fifty stations may be listed. This means that now a very small fraction of that random sample accounts for all the data collected for each individual station, and the smaller the sample used in any polling, the larger the error factor must be.

Now, consider that we have pages and pages of ratings data in each survey to show how each of the stations performs within specific segments of the population, defined by age group and gender. Because ratings companies print data showing how each of many stations ranks in size of audience in such narrow segments of the population as "men, ages 25 to 34, Saturday morning 6 to 10 A.M.," you can imagine how accurate that sort of data are going to be. In some surveys, you'll see the same "share" numbers repeating down a column or "share" numbers that are mathematical multiples of others in the same column. This tells you that very, very few respondents were measured in this segment of the audience. The error factor may be in a few hundred percent.

As program directors, what we need to understand about ratings is not only what they can tell us about the audience for our station and others, but also what they can't. We need to know what the statistical problems with ratings are. How much of what they tell us is real, and how much is "statistical noise"? All too often, stations change staffs (including their program directors) and formats, due to nothing more than a "bad book," which a little elementary analysis would have shown was very unlikely to be right.

Analyzing Ratings

Because we can't come to any conclusions about our ratings until we know how much confidence we should have in what they show, this section describes how to do basic ratings analysis.

The earliest form of radio audience research was based on telephone coincidental interviewing. Researchers dialed phone numbers at random and asked those who answered whether their radio was on and, if so, to what station it was tuned. When enough listeners were included in the survey, it was possible to project two figures: (1) the percentage of all households that had the radio on in each quarter hour and (2) the share, or percentage, of total radio listening that each network—later station—received. The second figure later came to be known as the average quarter hour share, and the telephone coincidental method was the only method of directly obtaining it. The resulting number, the percentage of total radio listening that each station receives, is often stated along with the average quarter hour rating, which is a percentage of the total population estimated to be listening to the station in the average quarter hour.

To understand the distinction between these, suppose that only 20 percent of the total population is listening to radio in any average quarter hour. A station with a 10 share of listening, the share figure usually quoted when discussing audience shares, has an average of 10 percent of the total average number of radio listeners in that time period (or "daypart"). However, because only 20 percent of the total population was listening to any radio station in the average quarter hour in this example, the average quarter hour *rating*, or the percentage of the entire population listening to the station in the average quarter hour, would be only 20 percent of that 10 share, or 2.0. Salespeople usually use ratings points in calculating advertising costs, but these numbers are usually too small to be of any real use in programming.

The C.E. Hooper Rating service used the telephone coincidental method into the sixties before the company disappeared—a victim of its inability to give either demographics or "cume" figures.

Cume—short for *cumulative*—is equivalent to newspaper or magazine circulation. It counts everyone who hears a station for five minutes or more during a week in the indicated time period, without taking into consideration how long they listened or how often. Although advertising agencies put a lot more weight on the share (because it attempts to report how many listeners might actually have heard a commercial announcement), cume is needed to develop a "turnover ratio," which can be useful for programmers as well.

The turnover ratio is simply the "cume persons" estimate divided by the "share persons" estimate. It tells how many times the audience turns over, or changes, on average in the time period. This figure can be used to calculate how many commercials must be run for a given client to reach the station's available audience. A common rule of thumb in the business is that the turnover ratio equals the number of spots that must be run to reach 50 percent of the station's cume.

This sort of calculation is referred to as "reach and frequency determination"—how many listeners are reached by how many commercials. For example, if a station's weekly cume is ten thousand people in the selected age group and the average-quarter-hour-persons figure in the same daypart is twenty-five hundred people—and if we're examining a four-hour daypart, such as 6 to 10 A.M. or 3 to 7 P.M.— the cume persons divided by the share persons would be 10,000 divided by 2,500, which would result in a turnover ratio of 4.

According to the rule of thumb, this means that four commercials, evenly spread throughout the daypart, should reach 50 percent of the cume, or five thousand people. More commercials should reach incrementally more people, but with decreasing efficiency because it would require running the commercial every five minutes to reach all of the cume, some of whom listen for very short periods of time.

This example tells the program director something useful: In this time period, the average listener (in the indicated age group) listens for one hour. We see this by inverting the calculation. Out of ten thousand listeners who tune in the station during the week in this time period, twenty-five hundred are listening in the average quarter hour: 2,500 divided by 10,000 is 0.25, or 25 percent. This means that the average listener is listening for 25 percent of the time in that daypart, which in this case is four hours. Twenty-five percent of four hours is sixty minutes, or one hour.

Unlike C.E. Hooper's methodology, ratings companies today generally obtain only cumulative information directly, and then they calculate the average quarter hour share by adding up all of the quarter hours listened to by all the listeners who listened to the station at all, and then dividing all those quarter hours by the number of cumulative listeners, to obtain the average listening span. Share is then derived mathematically using this formula:

Average Quarter Hour Persons = Cume Persons × (Average Listening Span [in Minutes] ÷ Total Minutes in the Daypart)

There are two things you need to understand before you make use of this sort of calculation. First, having had the opportunity of looking through three different survey companies' underlying data, from which the surveys are made, I can tell you that the average listening span (which, in our example, is sixty minutes) is composed of a handful of people who listen for nearly the whole four hours and a great number of people who listen for only fifteen to thirty minutes per day. So, any plans you make on how often to repeat certain music categories or other features—or how long to make uninterrupted music sweeps, for that matter—must take into consideration the shorter-than-average listening span of the *majority* of listeners, for maximum impact. That is, if you plan on having your airstaff announce music only every thirty minutes and if your ratings show an average listening span of sixty minutes, you may think that your average listener will hear two announcements. In fact, though, the majority of your listeners will probably hear no more than one announcement and—in a great many cases—none!

This is because of the second point you need to understand: Before ratings companies start to produce either the cume or the share figures, they modify the data by rounding it off in every individual case to the nearest fifteen minutes. Believe it or not, your station gets credit for a quarter hour of listening if a person listens for only five consecutive minutes in that quarter hour. However, if the person listens for four minutes or less, no credit is given at all. In fact, amazingly, if a person listens for five minutes, tunes out, and then tunes back and listens for another five minutes within the same quarter hour, the station will get credit for *two* quarter hours of listening—in the same fifteen-minute period!

So you see, if your "average listener" listens for sixty minutes per day in that time period, the majority of your listeners may be listening only fifteen to thirty minutes a day. In addition, because a listener is credited with fifteen minutes of listening based on only five consecutive minutes of actual listening, you can be sure that only some of your listeners credited with a quarter hour of listening actually listened the entire fifteen minutes and that a significant number of your listeners will have listened for only five or ten minutes per day.

How, then, can you establish station expectations or identity for people who are part of your cume but who listen for less than fifteen minutes per day? To start, you might want to schedule your breaks more often than you had planned!

However, we haven't yet decided how accurate your rating "report card" may be, and you really can't make intelligent programming decisions based on these figures until you understand that. (Unfortunately, for sales purposes, ad agencies usually don't care about accuracy as long as they have numbers to justify their ad-buying process.)

There have been many requests over the years for larger sample sizes in ratings studies. When so many stations are dividing so small a sample there cannot be sufficient confidence in each individual station's ratings to make intelligent use of them for programming. This can cause stations' ratings to wobble up and down from book-to-book, making ratings difficult for sales purposes too. Nonetheless, a larger sample size, though a good idea, won't solve the biggest problem with today's radio ratings. There are too many biases and too many departures from the requirements of the law of probability for the samples now used to be a true population cross section.

Understanding the Limitations of Ratings Data

To keep costs under control, ratings companies use sampling methods in which some "sample self-selection" can and does occur. That is, some members of the population are overlooked entirely because the sampling method doesn't include them, and among groups that are included, participation varies with willingness to participate.

To begin with, any survey that in any way uses telephones for sampling will exclude people who don't have telephones. Studies show that those who don't have telephones differ from those who do in various ways—by age, income, ethnic group, and lifestyle. Therefore, excluding nonphone homes will bias the outcome of the survey in favor of some stations and against others. Usually, it seems, ethnic and youth-oriented stations suffer the most from this telephone bias.

Of those people who do have telephones, some keep the number unlisted. If only listed phone numbers are included in the survey, people who are unlisted will be excluded. Studies show that the people who choose to be unlisted are different in various ways than people who choose to be listed. For this reason, all survey companies now try to include unlisted phones in their samples—with varying degrees of success. To whatever extent that unlisted homes are not properly represented in the survey, the data must be further distorted.

Of the people who are contacted by the ratings company, certain types and ages of people are more likely to cooperate than others, and obviously the cooperators are going to be the group represented in the survey. This further distorts the data and further weakens the data's validity in the very basis of such surveying—the law of probability. In the end, only those who are contacted by the survey company and who choose to cooperate constitute the segment of the population actually randomly sampled—and not only is that a smaller segment of the total population, but it is not a segment that can ever be represen-tative of the population as a whole.

So, should you program just to the people who cooperate in surveys, or should you program to everyone in your demographic target? Ideally, the latter. From a practical point of view, though, the former, but preferably without ignoring the latter.

Currently, the only fully national radio ratings company doing surveys through interviews conducted over the telephone is Willhight Research of Seattle (206-431-8430). They're the number two ratings service, based on the number of markets served. The company has a special strength in smaller markets due to their lower cost, but it is also attractive to large markets because of the availability of psychographic and product-user data cross-referenced to the ratings.

The number three ratings service is AccuRatings (800-777-8877), which is currently devoting its attention to developing its customer base in major markets. This company uses a controversial telephone interview technique that includes preference questions instead of simply behavioral questions.

The leading rating service is Arbitron (212-887-1300), which uses mail-distributed, self-administered seven-day diaries to record radio listening information. Because Arbitron gathers its data using diaries filled out by the sampled participants, you might think that it side-steps the problems associated with telephone surveys. Alas, that's not true. Arbitron uses a telephone-listing sample to place its diaries. In my opinion, this step further compromises their data. Here's how, based on my years of analysis and study. To begin with, because Arbitron starts with a sample of listed phones, the unlisted numbers are excluded. They obtain a second sample from each market, made by subtracting all listed phones from all possible phone numbers there, and then randomly choose a second sample from those. They then merge the survey data from both samples to compile each market's ratings report. The problem with this is that they cannot guarantee that they will obtain the same cooperation rate from the listed sample as from the unlisted one. To an extent, then, the two samples are not equivalent, and one can distort the results of the other.

Compounding the problem is that those who are intentionally unlisted tend to have different mind-sets and lifestyles than those who are unintentionally unlisted, so their cooperation levels are quite different, too. The unintentionally unlisted people are those who have moved during the past year; they're not in the current phone book, but they will be in the next one. Because they don't think of themselves as unlisted, their cooperation is similar to that of the listed sample. (They are similar to the listed sample, except that they are not as long-established in their address.)

On the other hand, those who are intentionally unlisted—those who pay extra not to be included in the phone book—tend not to cooperate when asked for their name and address by an interviewer who obviously doesn't know who they are and who has clearly dialed their number by chance. Would you provide this information? They're paying for privacy. If they won't tell the caller their name and address, they can't receive a diary and won't be included in the survey.

I conclude, then, that Arbitron's unlisted sample skews toward the unintentionally unlisted and that its participants tend not to be too different psychologically from those in the listed sample. If the intentionally unlisted are indeed underrepresented, this would undercount people who are less gregarious than others and who value their privacy, those who are very rich, and segments of the population that prefer to be unlisted. These people listen to radio, too, but might prefer different stations and listen in different patterns than those who cooperate in the survey.

To those who do agree to cooperate with Arbitron and who do provide a name and address, Arbitron sends a diary. In fact, the company sends a diary for every person in the household age twelve and over, thus clustering reported listening within households. The net effect, in my experience, is an average of about two diaries per household surveyed—and that average might be going up because Arbitron has been trying to improve its response rate from big households, netting more diaries per placement and reducing the cost of diary placement.

The problem with this is that even if every individual member of the household fills out his or her own diary without help—and I've seen studies showing that in at least some cases, one person in a family eventually fills out the diaries for everyone in the household—there is nonetheless some shared listening in family situations. I therefore consider that the effective sample size in an Arbitron survey may best be the "households surveyed" number and not the number of diaries in the survey—a substantially smaller number. I feel that, to eliminate this effect, there should be only one respondent per household.

Arbitron asks participants to fill out the diary to reflect actual radio listening for one week. Over the years, some published studies have suggested that the participants who actually record their listening *as they listen* may constitute as few as half or less of the total participants. In addition, these people may lose interest and log less and less listening as the seven-day week progresses. I find that it's widely assumed in the industry that the reason that Arbitron always starts surveying on Thursdays is to assure two good weekdays of data, plus enough information to generate weekend listening figures, and that any listening recorded for Monday, Tuesday, and Wednesday constitutes a bonus.

Of course, for those who might fill out the diary only after the week is ended, there is no such tapering off effect, but the respondents might tend to generalize their listening patterns—this is "recall" data—and list mainly the favorite stations they easily remember. This could benefit trendy and well-advertised stations, which are the most easily remembered, and it certainly could raise a cautionary flag about changing a station's call letters when a format is changed. Often, you are better off keeping the call letters that people have learned and just promoting a format change.

In my experience, there are a couple of other important problems to overcome with Arbitron data. The first is the Hawthorne Effect: When survey participants know in advance that they will be surveyed (such as when they receive a diary in advance), this foreknowledge could change their behavior. Because Arbitron is the only radio survey company that has ever given this sort of foreknowledge to their sample well in advance of surveying, it is uniquely vulnerable to this problem.

My second concern deals with the matter of the "cooperation" of the designated sample. At present, all survey companies have problems with cooperation because all start with telephones in some way or another, and as telemarketing has risen, cooperation has steadily dropped. However, because Arbitron is the only survey company that must learn the name and address of those they call (in order to mail them the diaries), Arbitron is uniquely vulnerable to that particular privacy issue. Also, because other surveys gain the raw listening data they need entirely through the initial telephone interview, it appears that only Arbitron has the additional problem of obtaining further cooperation from those who initially cooperated by accepting diaries but may not cooperate sufficiently to return them. It's a matter of record in every Arbitron report that only a fraction of those receiving diaries actually return them.

There are a number of other statistical problems with Arbitron data. Because the Federal Trade Commission regulates ratings companies not by requiring accuracy or even compliance with the law of probability, but simply by mandating that any flaws must be listed somewhere in their ratings books, you'll find in the back of each Arbitron report a long list of "limitations." I won't go into those here, but you should read that list and be aware of the implications.

To summarize, every ratings company fails to obtain a true cross section of the population. However, the leader, Arbitron, with its multistage requirements for respondent cooperation (initial telephone contact, attaining cooperation with mail placement, followed by the need for further cooperation to attain diary return) and with the difficulties posed by its use of multiple diary keepers in the same household is, in my opinion, the least accurate of the lot.

Drawing Constructive Conclusions from Ratings

One ratings book from a single survey period is, to say the least, inconclusive. It's best to average two or more books' data together, when there has been no format change, to increase the sample size and your level of confidence. Because the ratings have a definite impact on station revenue and often on the future direction of the station, it's very desirable to have regular access to more than one ratings service to obtain corroborative and contrasting data. If simultaneous Arbitron and Willhight surveys generally agree with each other, for example, then the reported programming trends and sales data may well be right. If they disagree, you not only have a warning about taking either survey too seriously, but you've doubled the chances of getting helpful sales data to maintain station revenue.

Of course, ratings aren't meaningless. You can learn from them. So now that you understand the limitations and problems of radio surveys, let's take a look at how you can use them for programming purposes.

The first and most fundamental thing to understand is that the cume figures for the station ought to be much more accurate than the share information. The cume represents an extraction from the whole survey's data, but the share is simply a mathematical derivation from the turnover ratio between cume and average listening span. (The share calculation is the reverse of the calculation shown earlier. You can use it to restore the data to an approximation of what the ratings company used to create the share data.)

What, then, is your station's cume in the demographics that you have defined as your target? How does it compare with the cume of competitive stations? Is there any trend visible in the cume over time? If the cume departs sharply from that given in the ratings books that preceded the present report and if there has been no major programming change that might account for it, the change is most likely a fluke.

The cume should be much less volatile than the share. The share is based on a smaller segment of the whole survey sample than the cume, and as an average, it is vulnerable to slight variations in the number of long-listening-span listeners within the sample. So, when there's no format or competitive change to explain it, a major change in the cume with no change in the share—or with a reverse change in the share—is almost certainly a fluke.

If the station changes its appeal, its listeners will listen for longer or shorter periods of time and will tune in more or less often, thus bringing about a change in the average listening span. However, cume is based on habitual listening. Only if the station completely changes its format will the "tuning-in habit" (cume) change quickly—and sometimes not even then.

Furthermore, if the cume changes sharply in one ratings book and the ratio of share to cume remains the same as before, this is almost certainly a fluke, and the cume should return to its normal level next time. The share drop caused by the cume loss should reverse next time as well.

If there is no station or market change and the cume drops but the share holds steady—or if the cume rises and the share holds steady or drops—chances are you are still looking at a fluke. When there have been no changes to account for it, the cume and average listening spans usually don't move in opposite directions. I've noted many times, though, the tendency of a cume fluke to be balanced by a fluke in the opposite direction in average listening span, so if the share figure shows significantly less change than the cume, the cume change should be an aberration.

All of this is nice to know when the cume (and share) have dropped. However, you must face the same probability of a fluke (and warn your general manager of it) when the cume (and thus share) increases suddenly and for no obvious reason! It's tempting to believe those "up" wobbles, but they usually lead to devastating drops back to normal levels in the next book—a disappointment that can easily destabilize the station, its staff, and your job, even though it's just a case of everything returning to normal levels.

Responding to Real Changes in Your Ratings

Up until now, most of my tips about the ratings have been focused on not reacting to a very bad (or very good) book. When can the ratings actually be telling you something real about a change in your audience? When you see a long-term trend in three or more ratings books from the same ratings company.

If the cume is relatively steady and the share figure is up or down significantly in one book, it could be a fluke in the average listening span data, but there is certainly the possibility that something is making the station more or less appealing to its core audience or that a significant competitor is cutting into the listening time of your cume. Whether such a share change really is significant won't start to become clear until a trend can be identified, and that requires at least one additional ratings report—and preferably at least two.

It's important to avoid modifying your programming because of a single bad book, even if the ratings drop undermines the sales effort and your general manager calls for immediate changes. If the audience change is simply statistical—a wobble in the ratings data, which the law of probability suggests is likely to occur regularly in radio ratings—any change you institute on the air in reaction to it will needlessly counter established listener expectations, which will tend to reduce the listening spans for real.

As I pointed out earlier in the book, you maximize average listening spans by maximizing frequency of "tune-in" and the length of time spent listening, and that happens when you clearly establish—and then consistently meet—listener expectations. So, even a good change in your programming can have the short-term effect of reducing your share figure until your cume gets used to it! Make programming changes only carefully and thoughtfully.

If a cume trend and/or a share trend upward or downward extends for three books in a row, it almost certainly is genuine.

By the way, if there is a programming change or a special promotion that leads to an upward-trending cume, expect to see your share figure actually drop at first because many of the new listeners will consider your station something other than a first or even second choice. The infrequent listening by your new cume will pull down your average listening span. The increase in cume may not fully offset the decrease in average listening span and thus may depress the share, at least until some of the new listeners change their habits and become regular listeners.

Because of the industry's tendency to concentrate entirely on share, programmers of mass-appeal stations are tempted to try to decrease music repetition and interruptions, hoping to reduce "irritation factors," extend their listening spans, and thus increase their share—but there is a danger in this. If the cume is going up or is large, the station is already appealing to a large number of people. That is, it is meeting their expectations, even if some actually prefer other stations; and even those marginal listeners tune it in (when they do listen) based on these expectations.

To be blunt about it, programmers hoping to extend listening spans on mass-appeal stations by installing longer music sweeps, by reducing identifiable station talk and jingle elements, and otherwise streamlining their stations to remove what they perceive as obstructions to longer listening are often removing the very elements that identify the station for its listeners and form the basis for the clearest audience expectations. If they're lucky, they just hurt their share but retain their cume. If they're not lucky, the share stays the same or increases, and the cume goes down. With a smaller cume, the share data—even if the numbers are larger—are less stable and more subject to wobbles, and of course, for sales purposes, the station's "circulation" has declined.

Here's an example. If a country music listener tunes in a pop station for its news coverage, its personalities, its energy level, or for a change of pace, that country listener is counted in the pop station's cume, but his or her intermittent listening reduces the pop station's average listening span and affects its share figure negatively—all resulting from the desirable gain of this country listener. Reducing the number of newscasts, the number of opportunities for the personalities to perform, or the energetic (intrusive) elements of the pop station, will cause this fringe listener to stop listening, instead of extending his or her listening span.

When the share is trending down but the cume is relatively steady, your audience is telling you that their expectations are not being met but they still like the station and hope it may yet live up to their expectations. If you change the overall thrust of the station, you will extinguish their expectations altogether, and the cume will follow the share downward. Instead, do some research, and identify your listeners' expectations. The changes you make should be toward responding to those established listener expectations; if you make your station what your listeners expect it to be, the cume will remain steady as the share starts to go up again. (The audience will be listening more often and for longer periods of time.)

One situation in which listening span just won't increase much no matter what you do to extend it is when the station derives a large percentage of its listening from in-car use. When much of your audience listens in the car, you cannot expect that they will drive more often or longer distances just to listen to your station. When they arrive, they turn off the radio and get out. Such stations must concentrate on building and holding their cume because when the listening span is inflexible, the only way to increase the average quarter hour share is to increase the size of the cume on which it's based.

A station with a large cume and a limited share due to this kind of audience usage should be selling with cume ("circulation"). If the average listening span is shorter than for other stations in the market that have smaller cume, that just means that the advertisers are going to have to buy more ads to reach your station's great big cume.

In fact, for *local* sales, if ratings are used at all, the cumes should be the only numbers used because they are the only figures that can be correlated with newspaper circulation figures.

As a former general manager and salesperson, I strongly suggest that ratings *not* be used for local sales, because what should matter most to a retailer is results, and numerical abstractions from inadequate mathematical studies do not necessarily relate to results. If a salesperson shows "average quarter hour persons" figures to a retailer, the merchant naturally compares them to newspaper "circulation persons," and the radio buy will look ineffective. However, when radio *cume* is compared to newspaper circulation, the two media look much more comparable.

To sum up, the best way to study ratings for programming purposes—in which your goal is to learn what is really happening in the market, not just what looks good for sales this time—the key is the cume. Does it wobble? Is it steady? Is it large or small?

In my ratings studies, I rank the stations by the cume in the demographic *and* 12+ (because, like it or not, the 12+ cumes are based on the entire ratings sample and thus should be the most stable). Then, for each station, I do the calculation I mentioned earlier in this chapter. I divide the "cume persons" into the "share persons" to get a fraction and multiply that by the minutes in the entire daypart being studied, to come up with the average listening span.

This listening-span figure inevitably varies from what it must have been in the original sampled data, because the ratings company has rounded any listening of five minutes or more in each quarter hour up to one full quarter hour of listening. But all stations in the book experience the same rounding, so the ratings data are nonetheless put back into perspective. Do make these calculations; if you only look at the share tables, you really have no idea what is actually happening to your audience—or whether *anything* is happening to your audience.

When you rank by cume, it becomes obvious which are the niche stations and which are the mass-appeal stations, and with these calculations the variation of listening spans for each type of station and the trending of these spans also become clear and understandable. Only when you understand what the ratings are actually telling you about your station and others can you make informed decisions about making changes in programming that will ultimately improve the station's position in the community and its billing. Only then can you be sufficiently informed to resist with logic the emotional demands of your superiors to make programming changes that are clearly unwise and counterproductive.

9

Working with Your General Manager

Your Boss, the General Manager

It would be nice for program directors if they could function autonomously, doing what they believe to be the right things to create and direct the best on-air product. Alas, they seldom can. In real life, the program director (PD) is responsible to at least one superior—the general manager (GM) or the station owner (sometimes the same person). This chapter is devoted to the PD's relationship with the general manager/owner.

You were probably hired as a program director by the general manager. If you were hired by the owner but work under the general manager, you probably have something to prove to the GM. Regardless of who hired you, you will be evaluated on your capabilities in your current position.

One of the common problems that PDs face is finding a way to gain the manager's confidence that they do keep the "bottom line" in mind. As a rule, GMs are promoted from the sales arena, and as a result, they frequently have a different way of looking at things than the most effective program directors do.

Because every station and every job situation is slightly different, the only way I can effectively counsel you about maximizing the relationship with your GM is to go into the psychology of the people involved and provide you with a way of better understanding yourself as well as the people with whom you work. The characteristics I'll give you will even help you identify and handle the exceptions. So, if you'll pardon me for it, I'm going to get a little heavy here for a minute.

The Psychology of the Individual

General managers are frequently outgoing and gregarious. They enjoy being a part of groups and in the center of the action and are often sports oriented. They tend to believe that others are like them and that others feel as they do about everything. (This is the origin of the so-called country club effect: the belief of some managers that because they, their families, or their friends don't like a given song or element of the programming, nobody does, and it should be eliminated.)

The sort of extroverted people I'm describing here frequently define themselves by their possessions, especially a very nice car, and they give as gifts what they want the recipient to have, rather than what the recipient might really want. They may not understand why anyone would need some time by themselves. They often wear their heart on their sleeve and are uncomfortable when it's necessary to keep a secret. (If this type of general manager is preparing to do something you won't like, he or she will become distant and will stop showing camaraderie with you.)

Turning to programming, the most effective PDs have to be able to get into the listener's head and perceive the station the way listeners do. This mandates the ability to see and understand the points of view of others. This ability is often associated with a somewhat introverted personality, sometimes with a less than compelling interest in spectator or social sports. These people often do not care a great deal about how others perceive them and may prefer to drive an unostentatious but practical car. They will give a gift that the recipient will want, rather than something that they would like the recipient to have. They feel the need now and then for periods of solitude, can keep a secret well, and tend to keep their emotions to themselves, perhaps even appearing cold or unfeeling as a result. (This can lead to a tendency for PDs to fail to balance routine critiques with enough positive feedback to the staff.)

It may have occurred to you that these two personality types also tend to represent the two personality types found in most successful marriages. In truth, opposites do attract in marriages, but they don't often attract in relationships between people of the same gender, as in a business relationship. Being such opposites, even though this is the most common situation, can lead to problems between a PD and a GM as they attempt to work together.

One additional characteristic of the most astute program directors is that they find psychological discussions like this one very helpful and illuminating. (Such discussions can help you gain insight into your listeners, too.) On the other hand, I've noticed that those who get impatient with this type of psychological discussion—considering its insights "obvious" or unnecessary—tend to be extroverted and less introspective people who have a hard time perceiving the station from various perspectives. (They often see it terms of industry clichés.)

A common difficulty in station management springs from a situation in which one or both executives involved are at the extreme end of the personality scale, as defined here. This is usually the result of a hidden feeling of inferiority. An extremely extroverted general manager tends to drive a very exotic, costly, or flashy car and often tries to dominate and intimidate subordinates. An extremely introverted PD tends to drive a very low status car and is unable to articulate the reasons for his or her programming strategies, working them out through intuition and what feels right. These may be the right things to do, but the PD cannot defend them with logic, which serves as evidence to the general manager that they haven't been thought through and are probably wrong.

Another characteristic of the extremely introverted program director is that he or she doesn't expect to be given respect and obedience by the staff and may act dictatorial, arbitrary, and unfeeling toward subordinates in an effort to establish and maintain authority. Needless to say, tyranny is counterproductive. Although this type of person may not believe it, all airstaffs (indeed, all teams of any sort) seek a leader and will automatically grant respect to their new PD right from the beginning—until he or she forfeits their respect through such conduct.

The moral is to never command through fear but rather to lead by example. If you have doubts about your course of action, don't reveal them to your airstaff; all teams want an assured leader. If you make a mistake, admit it; no team expects infallibility, and all respect honesty and openness in a leader. Just continue to lead with decisiveness after making any necessary course correction.

For this quick psychological overview of these types of personalities, I'm indebted to John G. Kappas at the Hypnosis Motivation Institute in Van Nuys, California (818-344-4464), to whom I direct you for more discussion on this subject. His book, *Your Sexual Personality*, is the most accurate and valuable work on human psychology that I've ever seen. It's applicable to everyone, not just those seeking success in romance. If you are interested in going into much greater depth on this psychological study, I suggest you obtain and read this book.

Building Mutual Trust

Now that you have a better sense of where your general manager may be coming from and perhaps have some new insights into yourself, let's turn to building the best working relationship possible between you and your general manager.

If your relationship with your GM follows the pattern described in the preceding section, you may fear that your manager does not grasp the need for consistency in programming and thus is willing to compromise elements of the on-air product for the sake of short-term revenue. Your stated objections to this may have already led your manager, in turn, to worry that you do not appreciate the financial responsibility of his or her position that in your naïveté you may act in ways that will unnecessarily cost the station money.

It's a bad start for the two of you to suspect the other's motives and agendas. You need each other's confidence. As the PD, you will have to go more than halfway to bring about mutual confidence. The GM may not really understand you, or the way you think, or what you are seeking to accomplish on the air. General managers of this type have difficulty understanding and trusting someone whose motivation seems different from their own. You, being more introspective, will have a much easier time understanding your GM than he or she will have understanding you.

In my experience, it is the general manager (GM) who sets the tone and style for the station, defines its ethical standard, its mission, and its objectives, as recognized and accepted by the rest of the staff.

Nonetheless, any lack of confidence between the GM and the PD can destroy any sense of "team" and can help create cliques on the staff. This is severely counterproductive to what the PD seeks to accomplish, making it essential that he or she make whatever effort is necessary to gain the confidence of the GM.

The single most important thing in gaining the confidence of your general manager is to display a businesslike attitude and mindfulness about the profit picture of the station. In my experience, program directors are often never told exactly how the station is doing financially and what its needs and goals are. From the time you take the job, you should ask. How can you help meet the station's objectives if you don't know what they are—or how far away from them you are now?

Second, as a program director, you may be expected to maintain an established programming direction—or perhaps you've been hired to make big changes. The usual attitude for PDs is, "Stand back and let me at it." Bad idea! If you're suited for the position, you probably have a much better idea than the GM right from the beginning as to exactly what should be done. However, you still need market information and the station background, which the GM knows well, and you also need the GM's confidence and backing in whatever you elect to do.

Thus your first step should be to sit down with the GM and discuss what he or she believes is right with the station and what needs improvement. What is the target demographic group? What is the target "psychographic" group? (Psychographics generally refer to lifestyle and attitude.) Why is the station doing what it is now doing?

If there seems no need to go so far as to change the format, what shortcomings should be addressed? If you were hired to make a format change, make sure that there is good cause for one, and then make a clear and detailed written plan for the proposed change. Get the GM's approval, present it to the sales department, and present it to your airstaff. Orchestrate its implementation, and make sure that everybody in the station is well prepared for it. The first impressions that your listeners get will be the lasting ones, and they'd better be good.

Also, learn about the station's heritage in the market. Every station is different, and how it was perceived in the past influences people's perceptions about what it is in the present. (Remember that listener expectations are based on past experiences with the station.) Talk to people in the community about the station. What do people know or remember best about it? What do they listen for? You may learn that something as seemingly incompatible as a news block within an intensive music format may be the station's "secret weapon" in the community and that eliminating it might do more harm than good.

Something else that you should ask the GM at the beginning of your term as program director concerns the budgeting. Will you have a role in this process? It is really no fun to go through the grind of preparing the next year's budget every autumn, but you're better off participating in the budgeting for your department if you can because nothing better puts you and your GM on the same wavelength concerning the financial goals of the station. Your participation in the budget process also makes a statement about your willingness to program the station in a businesslike way.

When I start a new position as program director of a station, I usually ask if I can be the one to sign the airstaff paychecks. If the GM doesn't object, this accomplishes the twin goals of showing your airstaff that they work for you and demonstrating that you have the confidence of your GM. Furthermore, if you are on the bank signature card for station checks, you can act as the backup signature for the accounting department when the GM is out of town, which is usually helpful. However, if your GM is not comfortable with this suggestion, just leave the thought on the table for a future time and accept the status quo. You want the GM's confidence, not his or her suspicion about imagined ulterior motives.

Make sure you keep your GM informed about what you are doing—on a regular, ongoing basis—and obtain his or her approval before you make changes in the on-air product. That makes it hard for anyone opposing your point of view to go around you to the GM with objections. An informed GM should back you up because he or she participated in the decision.

As noted earlier in this chapter, general managers are customarily drawn from sales because the station owners have to rely on the GM to maintain the station as a viable business. This means making sure that the station's income will meet or exceed all of its costs and expenditures each year. Naturally, then, most owners feel that someone with experience in sales should oversee the overall operation of the station. It is not unheard of today for a program director to be named general manager, but even such GMs have to supervise the sales department and make sure that the station is profitable. Naturally, it's hard to supervise a department that you don't understand.

Thus it is not simply for the purpose of maintaining staff harmony and having the confidence of the salespeople who sell ads in your programming that you will want to work well with the sales department. Your increased understanding of its operation and functions will be very helpful if you aspire to become a general manager. Working well with the sales department is the subject of the next chapter.

10

Working with Sales

The Sales Connection

The previous chapter addressed the contrasting personality types of those who are generally selected for the general manager and the program director positions. It discussed how these differences are often at the root of tensions, misunderstandings, and suspicions between these two key people. It explored what those differences tend to be and how the burden must usually be on the program director (PD) to make whatever extra effort is required to solve these differences.

Much of what we explored in the last chapter concerning the personality of the typical general manager (GM) also applies to the salespeople, from whose ranks the GM has usually come. Incidentally, a new GM is often put in a difficult position by such a promotion. All too often, the job of general manager is given to the top biller in the sales department as an inducement to make a long-term commitment and to help ensure a consistent billing pattern for the station. Yet both the GM and the sales manager should really be selected for their ability to lead their staff and not to compete with it. Leadership generally calls for a different personality and a different set of skills than found in the top billing salesperson.

Likewise, the program director job all too often is given to the best "jock" for similar reasons, and the same problems can arise. If you happen to have gotten your job as PD that way, you have the same

challenge ahead of you as many new GMs do: developing an understanding and appreciation for how the audience perceives the station
and how to be a leader rather than a competing member of the staff.
It'll take more work than you may have planned when you took the
job, but the result will be worth the effort.

The main point of tension between the sales department and the
programming department tends to center on the perceptions in each
department that their job is clearly the most important to the station's
success. Specifically, those in programming believe, with some justification, that without outstanding programming, the sales department
would have nothing to sell and that successful sales require a successful product. Meanwhile, those in the sales department are certain, with
some justification, that without their efforts, there would be no radio
station and that it is their work that pays the salary of every person in
programming, none of whom seems to them to be directly responsible
for a single dollar in revenue. Although salespeople will concede that
without programming, they would have nothing to sell, most have at
least a suspicion that they could sell even second-rate programming
and thus keep a revenue stream going regardless of what is broadcast.
(On the other hand, though, too often they blame difficulties in making
sales goals on deficiencies in the product or on shortcomings in the
size and quality of the audience attracted by the product.)

The Value of Being in the Loop

Generally, the key to good relations between programming and sales
is that the program director must make an effort to be at least an
"honorary member" of the sales team. The PD should try to attend
sales meetings. Doing so will not only be a tangible indication of the
PD's interest in providing a salable product to the salespeople and his
or her desire to be an asset to their sales effort instead of an impediment, but will also appear to the salespeople to be a tacit endorsement
by the sales manager of the importance of programming to the sale of
advertising.

In some stations, the sales manager does not want the PD to have
such tacit validation and might even see his or her presence in sales
meetings as a reduction of the sales manager's own power or authority
in the sales department. To avoid this sort of confrontation, it might be

best to suggest to your GM the value to the station's team effort—and to your own desire to help the station's sales effort—of your attending sales meetings whenever possible. If you obtain the GM's approval for this step before discussing it with the sales manager, there can usually be no objection to your presence. Arrange for your attendance at sales meetings in advance with the sales manager so that he or she can introduce you in the sales meeting and explain your presence there, easing your acceptance by the sales staff in their "territory."

Being a regular attendee at sales meetings will not only help you be perceived as an ally to that department, but will insert you into the planning process for promotions. Sales departments—and individual salespeople—have a tendency to dream up sales promotions that turn into on-air events and can be quite counterproductive to the programming effort. If you aren't in the planning loop, you'll find out about these promotions too late to stop them, even if you are supposed to have the authority to veto undesirable ideas before they are finalized.

One thing that you must try to avoid is saying no, except when absolutely necessary. Before turning down a promotional idea, for example, see if there isn't some way to modify it into a good station promotion from the listener's perspective.

Of course, an advertising client will like being prominently mentioned as the source or sponsor of a station promotion, but the client will gain more in the long run by being associated with a solid "station" promotion instead. That's because a promotion will have more credibility with listeners if it doesn't seem as though the station will prostitute itself and do anything for money. Thus the advertiser gains, too, when a promotion is properly structured. The planning and executing of every promotion should be oriented toward the station's listener and community goals, rather than simply an advertiser's goals. The PD is usually best at doing that—with the concurrence and approval of the GM, of course.

The Ad Standards of Successful Stations

In addition to generating insufficiently thought-out promotions, the sales department all too often schedules commercials that do not meet the standards of the station. It's generally up to the PD to catch these problems, which range from ethical and programming difficulties to legal obstacles. You'll need to establish your station's ethical and programming standards with the full agreement of the general manager and sales manager. If you do, your enforcement should not be difficult because you'll be backed up by both of these executives.

The fundamental ethical principle must be that the station will not knowingly broadcast a dishonest ad. This may seem to be just a noble objective, but in fact it is essential for maintaining the station's credibility with its listeners, and station credibility is really all the sales department has to sell.

Furthermore, the station must act as an advocate for its listeners in any dispute that arises between a listener and the client. The station may have many listeners, but if they begin to distrust what the station's ads tell them, they will stop responding to the advertisements—the death knell for repeat business.

Furthermore, the station must establish and enforce a standard on the length of spots. If the station carries a network, it may be necessary to require that spots are exactly the purchased length to fit the network availabilities. Otherwise, it may be reasonable to allow two seconds leeway per thirty seconds of commercial. Whatever the standard is, enforce it.

Having rules for spot length is important not only from the standpoint of discipline, good on-air production, and preventing an erosion of available time for music or other content in the hour, but also because only the length standard that is set and enforced can be required for political advertisements. An established but unenforced spot-length rule cannot legally be required of political "use" ads.

Another rule that I have always set and enforced at every station I've programmed is not allowing my staff announcers to read or record an ad that refers to the client in the first person—*I, we, our,* and so on. The reason for this is that every regular listener knows that this familiar voice works for the station and not the sponsor and that the use of the personal pronoun is therefore a lie. This raises unfortunate questions in the listener's mind: What else is this person lying about? Will the station say anything for money? The station's credibility—a priceless asset—is hurt as a result.

Isn't a policy like this asking for trouble? Maybe not. In my long career, I've never once had a sponsor question a copy change of *our* to *their* or to a repeat of the client's name, probably because the spot sounded right when changed this way and the client never noticed it. If a sponsor ever should question this policy, I'll always be ready to explain it. Clients often think that having the announcer use the first person somehow constitutes a desirable station endorsement of their business, but in fact it has the opposite effect of making it clear that at least part of the ad is untrue. Actually, when an announcer speaks knowledgeably about the client in the third person, the result is closer to a "station endorsement" of the sponsor!

The Lottery Rule

Two copy standards that have caused me some grief from the sales staff from time to time are the Federal Communications Commission (FCC) Lottery Rule and the Sponsor Identification Rule. For some reason, virtually all salespeople seem oblivious to these two rules, no matter how often they are warned about them, and the PD is usually the first and last line of defense for the station on both of these fully enforced FCC mandates.

The Lottery Rule has been particularly troublesome over the years. That's because the lottery mentioned in the copy is often the key reason why the sponsor is advertising in the first place, and the advertiser doesn't want to change it to make it conform to legal requirements. In addition, salespeople often don't want to risk the sale by going back and trying to get a change approved. Nonetheless, the station risks a fine amounting to thousands of dollars if the FCC catches an illegal lottery ad on the air, so it is your job to prevent this kind of jeopardy.

This rule essentially says that a station may not broadcast "information" about a lottery, except in certain circumstances. One of the exceptions is for legal state lotteries; this exception applies within the state in which the lottery operates. Stations outside of, but right along the border of, such a state often may advertise or promote the neighboring state's lottery, but it is best to establish in writing the legality of doing so with a communications attorney in Washington, D.C., before proceeding.

Making the situation more complex, an act of Congress in the late eighties created an exemption for certain private, nonprofit, and commercial lotteries that are not the principal business of the organizations conducting them. In every case, however, these lotteries are subject to the laws of the individual states in which the organizations operate. Instead of simplifying the rule as Congress intended, this act had the effect of making it a great deal more complicated.

Even the word *casino* in the name of a business may make the ad illegal because the principal business of casinos is gambling, even if the casino is legally operating in the station's state. What constitutes a legal lottery in your state? Is a permit needed? Can you verify that the business or organization does have a permit? It's a mess.

The only absolutely sure way to stay clear of violating this rule is to require that any promotion being advertised or publicized on your station is not a lottery. The way to do this is to stick to the old FCC rule and turn down any ad content for raffles, door prizes, and so on, except for legal in-state lotteries.

What exactly constitutes a lottery? A lottery is legally defined by the presence of three elements: prize, chance, and consideration. "Prize" is usually not an issue. Is there something to win? Few if any promotions that contain the other two elements have ever exempted themselves by making it clear from the start that listeners cannot win or gain anything by participating.

"Chance" is a much trickier element. If the promotion is truly a skill contest, then chance is not present. If, however, there is a drawing in case of ties at the end of a skill contest, there is an element of chance present. Any degree of chance at all in determining the winner of a skill contest establishes the presence of "chance."

For example, if paid spectators at a football game have the opportunity to try to win a prize by kicking a field goal at half-time, it may appear that the element of chance is missing because it takes skill to kick a field goal. However, unless there are auditions ahead of time, open to all spectators, to select those who are best at it for the opportunity of trying to kick the field goal, then there is probably an element of chance present in exactly which spectators are picked to have the opportunity to try the kick. This makes it a "chance" contest.

The third element that must be present to constitute a lottery is "consideration," which means that you have to pay to enter the contest. The FCC's current interpretation of consideration exempts money paid to a third party. If a free contest is held at a county or state fair to which admission is charged, there is no element of consideration if none of the admission money goes to the person, group, or company holding the contest. Postage or routine telephone charges are thus exempt (unless your own state's laws dictate otherwise). However, if the phone call involves a phone number for which the amount billed goes at least partly to the party conducting the contest—such as requiring participants to call a "900" area code or a "976" prefix—then consideration *is* most certainly present.

Consideration is also present when those who do pay to enter have a better chance to win than those who don't. An example of this situation is when a bottle cap is the winning token. If you can get one or two free bottle caps just by asking, but others can get as many bottle caps as they want by buying lots of the product—and if having more bottle caps gives you a better chance of winning—the legal advice I've received over the years says that consideration would certainly be present in this case.

Similarly, when a newspaper skill contest, in which an element of chance may be involved in determining the winner in case of a tie, requires obtaining the paper, you may have a problem. If a free copy is given to people asking for it only at the central newspaper office, but people can buy it at any newsstand, there is held to be an unequal opportunity for those who choose not to buy the newspaper, and consideration is again present.

You sometimes have to think like a lawyer when you are a program director. There will be times when your interpretation of the rules will be challenged and you'll need to have access to the station's legal counsel in Washington, D.C., for a legal opinion. Your right to consult this firm when necessary on matters like this should be established ahead of time with the GM because it does cost a few dollars to get a written opinion—and you really need to get the legal opinion in writing for your protection as well as the station's.

The Sponsor Identification Rule

The other FCC rule that program directors are usually expected to watch out for is the Sponsor Identification Rule. This was surely one of the first consumer-protection rules ever established by the federal government. Its purpose was to make sure that the powerful broadcast media always disclose to the public exactly who is paying to influence their behavior. The nonbroadcast press is not subject to any similar rules because that would constitute a violation of the First Amendment to the Constitution. The U.S. Supreme Court has endorsed some limitations of broadcasters' "free speech" with rules like this, with the rationale that licenses to broadcast are a limited commodity granted by the federal government and that the content of the broadcast must meet a "public interest" standard in choosing which applicant receives this potentially lucrative license.

It may seem logical that a sponsor should want to be clearly identified in an ad, but that's not always true. If the business or offer is not entirely honest, its sponsor might prefer not to be identified. If an itinerant promoter is holding a public event at a local venue, the promoter might choose to leave the impression that the owner of the theater or stadium is the one putting on the event. I've seen situations in which the advertisers of a commodity like milk will attempt to get away with not mentioning their sponsorship of the commercial. They want to leave listeners with the impression that their announcement reminding people that using their product is good for you is actually a station public service announcement rather than a paid ad. So be watchful.

This rule does allow a familiar brand name to serve as the sponsor ID if the maker of the familiar brand is in fact the sponsor of the advertisement. If it isn't, more is needed. A common violation is locally purchased national ads for soft drinks; they are usually sponsored by the local bottler. The rule specifies that the *right* sponsor must be identified! If there is more than one potential sponsor in the ad, the correct one must be clearly identified by such wording as "Sponsored by . . .", according to the FCC. Just as with the Lottery Rule, the commission enforces this rule with big fines.

The best person to catch a violation of the Sponsor Identification Rule is usually an on-air PD. If an improperly identified commercial has not been caught and fixed by the salesperson who sold it, it can slip through every other department of the station because everyone will assume that the spot was sponsored by the obvious name in the ad. However, even if the salesperson writes up the paperwork for the production department showing, for example, a famous soft drink name as sponsor, the contract for the advertising purchase will always show the correct information on where the bill goes, and program logs are prepared from the contract. So, if the label on the tape cartridge or the digital audio file shows something different than the official program log entry for the same ad, you can usually be quite sure that the sponsor is not correctly identified in the recorded ad and that the real sponsor is the one shown on the program log. Only somebody on the air, who sees *both* the log entry and the audio label simultaneously, is likely to spot the discrepancy.

Inadvertent violation of the Sponsor Identification Rule can happen at any station in any size market, and this is one of the most common FCC rule violations. I've repeatedly spotted and fixed the problem myself at every station at which I've ever worked, including at a top station in this country's number two market. Always be alert for this problem.

You may encounter a salesperson, sometimes even a sales manager or a general manager, who regards strict adherence to this rule, or to the Lottery Rule, as unnecessary "because there isn't an FCC office nearby." Of course, one reason to follow FCC rules is simply being a good broadcaster, worthy of the license. If that's not enough to enforce adherence to these and other FCC rules, there is also a very good practical reason: Most rule violations are called to the attention of the Commission by anonymous tips, frequently with an aircheck containing the violation. These tips come from competitors who want to make you squirm (or lose your job or destabilize your management) or from disgruntled present or past employees with similar motives.

Station violations can and have been caught this way even in the smallest and most remote markets. It's not worth the risk, particularly when the size of the potential fine is considered. Furthermore, an FCC sanction or two in the station's file can be a real handicap when the owner files for license renewal, particularly if there is a challenge for the license. You must take the FCC rules as seriously as the FCC does.

Making Yourself Invaluable to Sales

I suggest that you go beyond just establishing an ongoing relationship with the sales department through your participation in sales meetings and that you go beyond simply setting and enforcing standards that apply to ad copy. I urge you to assist in sales activities in which your own expertise is an advantage to the sales effort.

I've already suggested helping to plan promotions to meet station programming requirements as well as sales needs. How about writing commercials, too, as your schedule permits? Of course, avoid letting yourself in for more work than you can handle, but do be open to helping the sales staff on challenging copywriting assignments.

At most stations, the salespeople write their own spots. Unfortunately, they usually aren't very good at it. What usually passes for commercial writing is simply reducing the client's newspaper ad or copy notes to a few connected sentences that take the right amount of time to read aloud. Needless to say, this frequently results in ineffective commercials.

Writing a "Selling" Commercial

You should be considered the expert on writing good copy! What's needed to write good commercials is, to begin with, an idea of how to relate to what's in the listener's head. As I pointed out earlier, program directors are good at this—or they should be—and that's not a strong point with most salespeople. This section of the book reviews the principles of writing "selling" ad copy—a talent that should serve you well in preparing promotional announcements and other air copy.

What salespeople often overlook is that an ad cannot accomplish something if the copywriter doesn't keep the client's purpose in mind when writing the spot. All too often, salespeople just string together facts and slogans and hope for the best. Thus the first thing to do when sitting down to write copy is to identify the client's *goal*. What is the commercial supposed to accomplish? The second thing to do is to identify the most likely audience target. Who is the commercial supposed to reach?

The opening line of a spot is the most important part. If the opening line doesn't attract the attention of the intended prospects and point them in the direction the ad is going, they won't pay attention to the message until it's far too late. If the ad is to work, you must capture the attention of the "logical prospect" in the first sentence.

The second most important part of the copy is the ending. If the commercial is to get listeners to act, this is where it will happen. What do you want listeners to do now? Tell them explicitly. Retailers usually like to include everything they can in the spot, including both address and phone number. This can kill response. If listeners are expected to go to a store, include only the address and leave out the phone number. If they are to call, give the phone number and leave out the address. One or the other—never force a choice.

If the spot specifies an address, make it the last thing in the copy because if the listener will remember a specific detail in the ad, it will be the last thing they hear. Avoid street numbers; instead, use landmarks and cross streets when possible. Listeners tend to mix up numbers but can remember a location if they can picture it mentally.

It's a good idea to repeat any telephone number. If the ad requests a phone call from the listener, give the number the same way at least twice. The first time they hear it, they must decide whether they want to remember the number and call; if they do, the second time they'll concentrate on the number. Giving the number a third time will help listeners remember it.

Bearing in mind that listeners easily transpose numbers, you must make telephone numbers as simple to remember as possible. A common trick is to group numerals, so that 555-2374 becomes 555-23-74. Twenty-three is one number; seventy-four is another; so you've shortened seven numbers to five and made it harder to transpose, too.

The device of giving telephone numbers by making a word out of the letters that corresponds to the numbers on the telephone buttons can work, but if the word is misunderstood or easily misspelled, a listener can easily call the wrong number. If that happens, they won't try again. Also, letters are slower to pick out on the telephone buttons than are numbers. However, an easily understood and easily spelled word that represents the numbers to dial on the phone can sometimes help listeners remember that number long enough to call it.

The next question to ask when writing a commercial is why listeners should respond to it. Once you've got them sold on the product or service, why should they buy it from your advertiser instead of someone else? The reason why is called the unique selling proposition (USP). Every spot must have one, or it won't work. Identify the USP, and write the spot around it. If the sponsor has more than one USP, write separate spots around each one, and rotate the ads on the air. No spot will work if it has more than one main point.

If a client has a permanent advantage over the competition, one that can be stated clearly (perhaps in a slogan), they have a "position," and that is always the USP around which the spot should be written. For more on this concept, I refer you once again to the book *Positioning: The Battle for Your Mind* by Al Reis and Jack Trout.

After the opening line of the commercial and before the close comes the least most important part of the spot, the middle, but this should not be slighted either. The middle is where any needed detail goes and where the thought introduced at the start is expanded upon before "asking for the order" at the end.

From start straight through to its finish, the ad should be a clear and straightforward train of thought with no side issues or irrelevant material, even if the client provided it for the spot. As a copywriter, use your expertise to translate the client's needs into selling copy. Select the facts and organize the presentation in such a way as to deliver results.

If it isn't clear from the copy notes, ask the client what they expect in the way of results. A horde of people trampling in within the next three days? Or just a better image of the business in the public mind?

An ad that is intended as public relations, with no specific immediate result, is called "institutional." If the copy notes you're given seem to be institutional, leading you to write the spot that way, but the client claims later that it didn't work because no customers responded, you can't blame the client for the mistake of having written an institutional ad—you're the expert. Be sure you know what is expected, because you can't write the ad to achieve the client's goal if you don't know what that goal is.

If the commercial is expected to draw an immediate and tangible customer response, it must offer a reason to prompt such response: a specific event or offer. In addition, there should be a time limit within the copy for responding to it so that the response will occur within the necessary time frame.

Briefly, these are the basics for good commercial writing. There is a great deal more to say on the subject, but that's outside the scope of this book. If you follow these key principles, using them as a checklist when you sit down to write commercials or promos, you should write effective broadcast copy. This ability is a solid bit of expertise that you can offer the sales department in the interest of making the entire station staff an effective team with a single goal: being the best radio station in the market!

11

Working with Engineering

Being Involved in How Your Station Sounds

The frequently adverse relationship between programming and sales is legendary and often overstated. However, there is another relationship involving the program director (PD) that sometimes borders on being frustrating, and it need not be. That's the PD's relationship with the chief engineer.

Frequently, the PD feels that the station doesn't sound as good as it could. This is a legitimate programming concern because although the programming is considered to be the content of the broadcasts, the way the station sounds can definitely affect listeners' reaction to the station. However, the chief engineer (CE) is frequently suspicious of the PD's motives in wanting to change the sound of the station and fears that the PD wants to "junk up" the sound. The result, all too often, is mutual suspicion, with the CE stalling—nodding agreement but making no changes—secure in the knowledge that the PD doesn't know how to achieve the sound that he or she is after. As I said, the relationship need not be this way.

Actually, the PD and the CE have many common goals; unlike others in the station management, their primary interest is in how the station is perceived by listeners. This should bring them together, without each fearing that the other is encroaching on his or her territory. Most CEs are a lot more concerned with the sound of the station than the content, and PDs are mainly concerned with the content; they simply want the technical sound that the station transmits to be competitive if not superior to that of other stations in the market.

Once the CE is satisfied that you want to make him or her a partner in getting the sound of the station right, rather than trampling on his or her judgment about how the station should process its audio, then the relationship generally becomes quite productive. I've only encountered one CE in my many years in the business who felt threatened by a programmer taking an interest in this—and he needn't have. I still have no idea how to build or fix the equipment. I *need* the help of a superior engineer.

You may have heard the saying, "You don't have to be a watchmaker to want to learn how to use a watch." The chief engineer is the watchmaker; the program director is the user. It is legitimate and natural for the CE to work with the PD to achieve the sound the programmer wants, as long as it is consistent with good engineering practice.

There was a time when programmers wanted heavy audio limiting and compression for loudness and to impart "energy" to the broadcast, whereas the CEs quite rightly preferred not to ruin the quality of the audio with "pumping" and distortion. Nowadays, though, the tendency is for both parties to want the station to sound "clean" but competitive, which should lead to a natural partnership.

The use of heavy limiting and compression adds distortion to the signal. This can, under some circumstances, sound exciting, but it nearly always increases listening fatigue in members of the audience—particularly older ones—leading to shorter average listening spans. Furthermore, the rise of compact discs (CDs) and digital sound has been slowly educating consumers to recognize and want clean, undistorted, high-fidelity sound. This, in turn, has led to new generations of audio-processing gear that strives to reduce dynamic range and properly level all programming while still sounding as if there were no processing at all.

The Evolution of Modern Audio Processing

Let's pause a moment and tip our hat to the father of modern audio processing, George M. Frese of East Wenatchee, Washington, whose studies of broadcast audio in the fifties and sixties led to his remarkable, hand-built Frese Audio Pilot. Though still little known in the business, Frese invented a computerlike device that introduced nearly every innovation in modern audio processing, including controlling enormously wide dynamic range instantaneously and inaudibly, with the speed of gain change controlled by program content; "gating" so that background noise didn't get pulled up in moments of silence; asymmetrical peak switching; soft, wave-shaped "peak clipping" for maximum program density; and equalization—in other words, audio processing with an "unprocessed" sound.

The Frese Audio Pilot also incorporated one thing that is still unique to this historic device: output-monitored audio processing via a return line from the transmitter. This enabled the unit to be set to deliver exactly the desired modulation parameters and provide exactly the type and percentage of modulation desired. It controlled the two peaks of the wave separately, based on feedback from the actual transmitted wave.

Frese's invention was a true "audio computer," and it inspired a generation of equipment designers, including one whom I'm pleased to know personally, Donn Werrbach. His Aphex audio-processing devices mimic many of the Audio Pilot functions, though they use different and novel techniques to achieve them. Because Frese didn't patent any of his inventions, he receives no financial benefit from the audio-processing industry he inspired, but we can at least acknowledge his contribution.

Maximizing Audio Processing

If you're going to work with your chief engineer to get the station sounding the way you want, you'll have to understand the basics of how and why audio is "processed." You may not realize it, but all radio receivers contain an automatic volume control (AVC) circuit, which maintains the same subjective volume level for all signals received, regardless of whether they are strong or weak. As a result, the subjective loudness of a station is a function of the programming presented and especially the way it is processed, rather than the strength of the received signal.

Thus audio processing is important to all stations, and audio compression is fundamental to such processing. If a transmission is to be easily heard at normal listening locations (especially cars), it must be "processed" to reduce (or "compress") the dynamic range. Dynamic range is the ratio of the softest sounds to the loudest.

Alas for audio purists who deplore any processing at all, even a small drop in level of 6 dB (equal to the volume difference between 0 VU and −6 VU on a standard control board VU meter) is enough to make a station inaudible for most listeners because people tend to listen to radio in noisy environments. To keep the audio peaks from dropping even that much during normal programming, the basic tools of the radio station are a compressor and a limiter, used one after another in that order. Let's take a look at what they do and how they do it.

Superficially, both of these devices seem about the same. Each is a level-controlling amplifier. From a practical standpoint, though, they work quite differently. The compressor is designed to take whatever audio signal is being sent to the transmitter and adjust the level (volume) inaudibly so that the peaks of the audio are held within a fairly narrow range. Portable cassette recorders and CB radios are just two devices that usually have automatic gain control built in, which means that the input volume does not have to be manually set; it's done automatically by a compressor.

However, the compressor does not act speedily enough to keep occasional instantaneous peaks from shooting quite a bit above the average level it sets. As a result, if the only thing you use to control the loudness of the audio going into the transmitter is a compressor, the average level of the broadcast will be kept a lot lower than you'd like to have it in order to avoid having those occasional peaks "overmodulate" the transmitter and cause distortion in the receiver.

To allow the average audio level to be about the same as the peak level, there must be a limiter following the compressor. This device does not affect sound below a certain level, or audio threshold, which is adjustable. However, when any element of sound—even a very quick peak—exceeds that threshold, it instantaneously turns down the level enough to keep that peak from getting any louder than the preset threshold level.

The limiter is usually set so that the average peak level from the compressor pushes slightly above the threshold, causing 2 or 3dB (or VU) of continuous limiting and stopping all peaks from exceeding the preset level. This permits a higher average level of audio to be fed to the transmitter. If the compressor audio were to be driven harder (higher) into the "limiting," the audio density would increase. This makes the station sound louder at the cost of reduced dynamic range, and with older equipment, it causes more distortion of the audio.

Modern audio processing often mimics Frese's "soft clipper" concept by using an audio-clipping device to flatten off the top of the wave peaks; this can allow even higher audio density and "loudness" than the compressor-limiter combination can achieve, by bringing the average level even closer to the peak level. However, this often occurs at the cost of increased undesirable distortion, which the listener calls a fuzziness or "buzziness" in the sound. If the listener notices the audio processing's effects, you can be sure you're overdoing it.

In general, audio processing should be set for the maximum loudness and audio density short of where distortion and other artifacts start becoming even slightly noticeable. A high average modulation level not only keeps the station competitive with other stations when tuning across the dial, but it can actually maximize the coverage area of the station.

For AM (amplitude modulation) stations, what's being used to encode the audio information on the signal is a variation of the amplitude, or strength (the power in watts), of the signal. For this reason, there is actually more power leaving the transmitter on the positive peaks, and high positive peaks (within FCC limits) can improve the signal-to-noise ratio of the signal in the fringe areas.

For FM (frequency modulation) stations, in which the frequency of the station (the actual dial position) is what is varying to convey the audio information to the receiver, the much higher frequency "smaller" radio wave bounces off mountains, buildings, and metal objects, causing multipath distortion. Dense modulation on FM stations can reduce this type of distortion in the receiver and can extend the usable signal into areas where reception is difficult.

Your chief engineer might have some difficulty accepting that denser modulation could actually accomplish this for FM stations, but side-by-side comparisons by professional engineers have shown that the improvement can be quite significant. In addition, dense modulation also improves the signal-to-noise ratio of FM signals. However, high modulation density will not have any useful effect in forthcoming digital broadcasting, in which audio processing will only be needed to keep the broadcast audible over ambient background noise where people listen.

To avoid confusion, I should add that in digital broadcasting, digital compression is totally unlike audio compression. Digital compression is the technique of making a digital bit stream broadcastable within a manageable bandwidth by eliminating the parts of the audio data that would not be audible for various reasons. This can cut the digital data by as much as 80 percent, preferably without loss of audio quality.

Returning to audio, though, modern audio processing includes more than simply controlling the volume, or level, of the broadcast. There are sophisticated techniques available to radio stations today to further modify the sound to make one station sound different from another and to improve audio clarity. The most common of these involves adjusting the tonal balance of the audio, or "equalizing" it.

Before you embark on your odyssey to achieve the best possible tonal balance, or equalization, of your signal, you must change the way you think about sound. Your concept of sound probably derives from the audio systems in your home or car, but this can mislead you when tailoring radio station audio.

You see, consumers can turn up the bass, adjust the midrange, tweak the treble, and get the sound exactly the way they want it with ease. It's much harder doing this for a station because you are stuck with a firm limit to the overall maximum sound level you can transmit.

If you turn up the bass at home, the midrange and treble can and do stay as they were. This is not so in radio transmission. If you boost one section of the audio spectrum, other parts must drop because you are changing the audio energy balance throughout the whole acoustic band of frequencies, altering the relative levels of each part of the audio spectrum.

In broadcasting, where there is a maximum level that you are always trying to stay near, the compressor and limiter combination will keep pulling up the newly equalized audio to hold it at the same maximum level as before. This means that you are actually turning down some parts of the audio band when you want to make other parts more prominent. In practice, that's a considerable difference. To bring up the midrange, you are in effect turning down the bass and treble. Likewise, to emphasize bass, you must reduce the midrange and treble, and so forth.

If this distinction is not yet clear, visualize it this way: Compare your radio signal to a full drinking glass, containing three layers of differently colored fluids, each of which stay separate and distinct. The blue layer on the bottom is bass, the yellow layer in the middle is midrange, and the red layer on the top is treble.

Now, beside it, imagine your home audio system as a very big drinking glass that you hardly ever fill up; these three fluids stay rather low in that glass at all times. So, when you want more bass at home, you just pour in more blue fluid, and there's still plenty of room in the glass to accommodate the new, larger layer of blue fluid without removing any of the other two layers.

For broadcasting, we keep the three fluids right up at the top of the glass at all times to achieve the best competitive loudness and coverage. When we add more blue fluid, we have to take out some of the other two colors of fluid so there is less of those in the glass. You want more bass in your signal? You're going to have to lose some midrange and treble. Do you really want to do that?

In fact, most PDs do seem to want more bass in their signal—and sometimes more treble to balance it out. This works against the goals of the station, though, because most consumer radios have weak bass. ("Aha," says the PD. "That's why I want more bass.") The result, on these poor receivers, is that the radio can't reproduce the strong bass at anywhere near full level (and, worse yet, distorts it on the average radio, making the station sound muddy). Because the extra treble you added to counter the heavy bass is being boosted at the expense of the midrange—the section of the spectrum that we hear best and that most radios reproduce best—the station sounds muddy, shrill, and actually lower in average volume than the competition.

However, if we enhance just the midrange frequencies that we hear best, the station may sound competitively louder, but it may also sound "nasal" and unbalanced. The goal is to achieve a distinctive sound balance that sounds good on a wide variety of receivers while remaining competitively "loud"—and this is really the test of a good chief engineer.

Multiband processing, a tool developed in the sixties and seventies to help accomplish this, is today a very common part of stations' audio chain. A multiband processor is a compression device that first splits the audio spectrum into two, three, or more bands, in much the same way as tone controls do, and then compresses each band separately. In effect, it's an automatic equalizer. It brings up the bass on sources with weak bass and likewise adjusts the midrange and treble to keep the audio balance consistent from source to source, regardless of what sort of audio the station is broadcasting at any given moment.

The multiband processor not only keeps the audio balance of the station consistent, but by careful adjustment of the output levels of each individual band, it can maintain a desired balance of the audio spectrum, as you, your general manager, and your chief engineer mutually decide is best after many listening experiments. (This listening must be done on typical radios—not on super sound systems.)

Other types of sophisticated audio devices may be added experimentally to the processing—including stereo expanders and harmonic-generating devices that can restore overtones eliminated in recording and broadcasting and thus make the music sound more "live." It's important to make sure that you actually hear a practical difference using one of these expensive gizmos in a side-by-side comparison in and out of the circuit. If you can't hear it when listening intently in a direct A/B comparison, it probably has no useful effect upon your listeners at all and should be discarded.

One additional type of processing device that can be very helpful in tailoring a station's sound is a fixed equalizer—but it must be used very carefully. There are two basic kinds of equalizer: the graphic and the parametric. A graphic equalizer, the kind usually sold to home and auto hi-fi buffs, has a series of vertical sliders, each representing one octave of sound or a fraction of an octave. There may be five, ten, twelve, twenty, or more bands of tone control available, stretching from the deepest bass to the highest treble.

This device is called a graphic equalizer because the setting of the individual sliders forms a sort of jagged horizontal line—a "graph" of the bass-to-treble tonal balance of the sound. Graphic equalizers are very helpful in a production room, allowing correction of the tonal balance of recorded commercials, which all too often are somewhat deficient in audio quality. It can also create special effects for staff-produced spots.

However, the multiband processor is designed to accomplish automatically what a graphic equalizer does manually so you usually won't need one of these in your audio chain to the transmitter. What you might instead choose to use between the compressor and the limiter is a parametric equalizer, so named because you can set the parameters for the part of the audio spectrum to be adjusted. One parameter would be the center frequency of the audio band to be adjusted; another would be the width of the audio band you've chosen; and the third would be the degree of boost or reduction in that band.

Because any adjustment of the audio using a parametric equalizer will still be subject to the "full drinking glass" phenomenon mentioned earlier, meaning that you will reduce some audio frequencies when you boost others, any work done with this device should be kept relatively subtle. Here are a few things you can do with a parametric equalizer.

To enhance perceived clarity of the overall station sound, including the voice clarity of your announcers, set the audio band in the midrange—around 3,000 Hz. Set the bandwidth to "narrow," and try setting a boost of perhaps 6 dB. Then tune the center frequency slowly between 2,000 Hz and 4,000 Hz while listening on a variety of radios. You should find a center frequency that gives the station an open and very up-front sound without creating a harshness or a nasal quality with voices. Adjust the degree of boost on that audio frequency for the best overall bass-to-treble balance.

If you have a couple more bands of audio to work with on your parametric equalizer, consider adding a 2- or 3-dB bass boost around 120 Hz—and then rolling off all bass below about 70 or 60 Hz. This can add more apparent "bottom" to your signal while reducing the total bass energy, thus avoiding the fuzzy, distorted bass and weak midrange effects of a real bass boost. (Your transmitter might like the result better, too.)

With your third band, you might try a gentle, gradual roll-off of highs above 10 kHz (for FM only; AM is not permitted to exceed 10 kHz in treble response anyway) to reduce the distortion effects of modern high-frequency FM processing. Such a treble roll-off won't be necessary in digital audio broadcasting, but the other two adjustments described might be.

Concerning the rationale for a treble roll-off for FM, I should explain that there's a wicked treble boost built into the FM transmission process, which is matched by an equal roll-off of treble response in all receivers. This was intended to reduce the perceived hiss and noise in the high frequencies when FM was perfected in the thirties by its inventor, Major Edwin Armstrong. However, today's hot highs from compact discs create terrible transmission problems for FM stations because of that automatic treble boost. As a result, severe treble reduction and clipping is built into modern FM audio processors to permit high average modulation without overmodulating the highs. This causes distortion and graininess in FM stations' treble range, and rolling off the treble fed to the transmitter can clean up the station's sound by causing less severe audio processing.

Because with all of the adjustments I've discussed making with a parametric equalizer, you are enhancing narrow bands of frequencies, there is relatively little energy added to the overall processed sound of the station after the multiband processing (very little "fluid" added to the "drinking glass"), minimizing the problems of balancing each part of the audio spectrum against one another. However, make sure that you place any parametric equalizer *after* the multiband processor, so that the equalizer's enhancements are not systematically reversed by the processor!

A Few Warnings

I've given you the basics of audio processing and adjusting the sound of your station to help match your vision of how the station should sound. However, I have a couple of important warnings.

First and foremost, you should work with your CE on such adjustments. In fact, let him or her do the actual adjustments. If you have succeeded in being accepted as the CE's sidekick in polishing the station's sound, you two can be a very effective team, but the equipment is the CE's province, and he or she should supervise any adjustments.

On the other hand, if your CE would rather not have you giving input on the station's sound and audio processing, discuss your objectives with the general manager and obtain his or her approval for your goals. If the general manager endorses what you want to do, you should be able to get it done. Promise to keep your hands off of the machinery and to limit your participation to providing comments and suggestions! I hope the preceding section will enable you to make effective ones.

The second warning concerns how we all hear what we expect to hear. We must not lose sight of how the station is perceived by its listeners. I have seen otherwise intelligent PDs get so involved in "tweaking" the station's sound to match a sound in their head that they haven't been able to step back two paces and hear how truly awful the overall effect has become. Listen on a variety of radios, and notice not only the details, but the overall effect of your station in the competitive picture.

I've warned you to keep your hands off the processing gear and let the CE do the adjusting (with your input, of course). Most CEs are very firm about this because they are personally responsible to the general manager, owner, and the Federal Communications Commission for the legal operation of the station and the maintenance of the equipment. If they find the processing set up differently from the way they had it, they feel as violated as you would if the chief engineer had gone into the control room and made some change in your music rotation or your liner cards without asking you!

Once you've demonstrated fully to your CE that you can be trusted, you may be able to get his or her approval to make minor adjustments on your own after you have had a chance to do a lot of listening to the station. If you do get that permission, that's useful, but don't abuse it. Leave the CE notes explaining just what you did so that he or she is always fully up-to-date on what you've done and why—and has the opportunity of sharing his or her input on it with you.

Quick Fixes That You Can Do

More and more, stations are using "contract engineers" as their chief engineers. These multiple-station, part-time engineers have been a staple in smaller markets for decades, but now they can be found in even large markets. They are under contract for scheduled weekly maintenance, plus emergency work when the station is off the air, regardless of the day or hour. If your CE is a contract engineer, you may not see him or her around very much.

Under such circumstances, I've had to learn quite a bit about doing emergency maintenance myself, although I'm still not able to diagnose or fix a circuit or electronic component. If something quits working when no engineer is at hand, either you will have to save the day or you will have a real problem on your hands. I've discovered that at least 90 percent of the time, what needs fixing is something that a program director can do.

For example, if there is a big hum in the audio, look to see whether a ground wire has come loose somewhere on that input. (If it has, the hum you hear is referred to as a "ground loop" hum.)

If a piece of equipment has stopped working, see if it's still plugged into the electric socket. If it is, see if it has a fuse—usually inside a round black plastic cap sticking out of the back of the unit (that's a fuse holder). Push in the black cap and twist it clockwise part of a turn until it releases, pull it out with the fuse in it, and see if the wire visible through the fuse's glass tube appears to be intact. If not, the fuse needs to be replaced.

There is another way to check the fuse: If you have access to a volt-ohmmeter, switch the meter to "resistance" and check the meter by touching its two probe wires together. You should get a full-scale or "zero resistance" reading. Then check the fuse by touching the two probes against the opposite metal ends of the fuse. This should give you the same "zero resistance" reading; if it doesn't, the fuse is bad. Volt-ohmmeters are very cheap at electronic-supply stores; you may want to buy yourself one. They're handy to have for purposes like this.

If the fuse is bad, replace it. If it's okay, put it back in its socket by pushing the fuse holder cap—with the fuse in it, as you found it—all the way back in, and turning it counterclockwise until it stops and locks down.

When a large bank of equipment is down, find the station's power panel and see if any of the electric circuit breakers are blown (the switch would be part way between on and off). Flip any blown breaker switches to off then back to on. If it blows again immediately, something has shorted out on the circuit. Unplug everything you can on that circuit, reset the breaker, and if it stays reset, return to the affected area and start plugging things back in one at a time. At some point, you should blow the breaker again. Unplug the last device plugged in—that's the shorted unit—and reset the breaker again. You should be able to plug everything else back in and reset the breaker. The shorted item will have to be removed for the engineer's inspection. Leave a note with it describing the problem.

If a tape recorder, cassette machine, or cart machine starts to sound dull or weak or even stops reproducing sound at all, first try cleaning the heads—the metal blocks that the tape runs across as it plays. Isopropyl alcohol, with as high a percentage as possible (99 percent is best), scrubbed over these heads with a cotton swab, will clean off the dirt. If dirt is the problem, you'll see it on the swab.

If audiotape starts playing back with no highs and a weird "flanging" acoustic effect, the head azimuth has become misadjusted; the tape head is no longer absolutely perpendicular to the path of the tape. There's a screw adjustment beside the head itself, often sealed with a drop of fingernail polish, and in an emergency it can be adjusted carefully with a small screwdriver while you listen to the tape play back in mono through the cue system. Turn the screw until the highs become as clear and bright as possible. However, it's best not to do this yourself until you contact the CE and get approval to try. The CE may want to do it personally; if not, the CE will want to know later what you did to fine-tune the azimuth adjustment.

Sound "cutting out" in headphones means that a wire has broken in the cable between the plug and the headphones or has come off in the plug. If you know how to solder and have access to a soldering iron and a roll of electronics-type solder, you can unscrew the plug cover and fix any broken wires inside. If a wire is broken in the cable between the headphones and the plug, you may be able to find the bad spot by carefully twisting the cable in sections, one narrow segment at a time, while listening. If you find the bad spot this way and are confident in handling a soldering iron, you can try slicing out the bad section and carefully soldering the two or four delicate, flexible wires in the cut ends back together. Then seal and support the new joint with electrical tape. Otherwise, just change the headphones and leave the repair to the CE.

If you see odd readings on any of the station monitoring equipment, take it very seriously. You probably can't fix any transmitter problems and shouldn't try to, but odd readings may very well mean a major problem in the transmission system. Immediately contact the chief engineer or the general manager about what you've noticed, and then leave it to them to decide what to do. Your job as an operator is to spot and report the problems. It's the job of the "chief operator" (chief engineer) and/or the general manager of the station to decide what action to take.

If the transmitter appears to be operating improperly and you cannot immediately reach the chief engineer or general manager, seriously consider taking the station off the air until you can reach them for advice. It is hoped that you'll be able to reach one or both without delay and won't have to make this agonizing decision by yourself, but if push comes to shove, the equipment and the license are more important than staying on the air.

You may be criticized for signing off the transmitter in a case like this, but let me tell you from (alas) personal experience that it's nothing compared to what will happen to you if you decide to leave the transmitter on despite the odd readings and then a key or expensive component burns out or catches fire! You're always better off assuming that the station monitoring equipment is exactly accurate and reporting any discrepancies immediately. (Be sure to note them on the transmitter [operating] log, too—along with the name of the person you notified about it.)

To summarize, if you develop a cooperative relationship with a really good chief engineer, this team will constitute a real competitive weapon in fine-tuning the sound of the station. As a result, you should have a great-sounding radio station. Meter readings and log entries are made not only for the chief engineer but also the F.C.C. You have specific responsibilities involving the Commission too, as we see next.

12

The FCC and You

The Importance of Taking FCC Rules Seriously

Broadcasters sometimes look upon the Federal Communications Commission (FCC) as a very distant traffic cop, a bureaucracy that is more or less benign and whose rules do not require undue concern. This is a terrible mistake.

It is true that the FCC seldom intends to get really nasty with licensees. To its credit, the Commission tends to assume that each station is doing everything the way it's supposed to—until it learns differently. However, when it does learn differently, it can get really unpleasant: large fines and even the loss of a license on occasion. There are two main ways in which the FCC discovers wrongdoing: through routine inspections and through complaints.

The Commission eventually inspects every broadcast station, usually without prior notice. When the inspectors walk in, the personnel at the station visited frequently warn other local stations in the hope that the favor may be returned someday. However, the inspectors are aware of this networking, and quite often these days they may choose not to visit any of the other stations in the locality just then. They really want to get a snapshot of the station they are inspecting as it normally operates.

Sooner or later, the inspectors from the regional FCC office will walk in on you. If your station is in a remote area, far from an FCC regional office, you may think that you're relatively immune to a

165

surprise inspection, but you are not. All stations are eventually visited. I hope for your sake that the FCC will not find serious violations during its visit of your station. The Commission's fines tend to run between $2,500 and $20,000, but Congress has authorized fines of up to $250,000 for each individual offense, and now and then in egregious cases the Commission will assess as much as that. The FCC does not have a collections department, but when a fine is not paid, the Commission turns the matter over to the U.S. Department of Justice for collection.

There is one other way that the Commission learns in timely fashion of violations that can cause you lots of grief, and it works just as well in remote markets as in major ones: complaints. The Commission accepts and acts on complaints, regardless of whether they are signed or anonymous and regardless of whether they have come from a citizen or a competitor. The majority of complaints about stations come from other stations—for competitive and even malicious reasons. Those are the unsigned ones. If the complaint is about something you broadcast, there will no doubt be a tape cassette included with the complaint.

Are you taking the rules seriously yet?

Important FCC Rules

You are responsible for making sure that all programming-oriented FCC rules are being observed by the staff at your station. We dealt with two of these rules in Chapter 10: the Lottery Rule and the Sponsor Identification Rule. The violation of these two rules can usually be traced back to the actions of salespeople, but these are programming rules, and it's vital that you prevent these problems before they occur. The station ownership and management will generally blame (and fire) you when the FCC acts on violation of these rules. The following programming-oriented rules are in effect at this writing.

Station Identification

A station identification (legal ID) is required when a station signs on the air, signs off the air, conducts equipment tests, and once hourly—

as close to the top of the hour as possible. It must consist of the station's call letters, followed immediately by the "city of license," as shown on the station's license. The license must be posted at the transmitter control point. Any other city or cities may be mentioned in the ID, but only after the city of license. (The only things that can legally come between the call letters and the city of license in the legal ID are the station's frequency, or dial position, and the name of the owner of the station, as it appears on the license.)

Logging

Although the FCC does not presently require that a station have a "program log" to schedule the commercials and program elements and show that they've run, in practice very few stations can get by without one because a completed log is usually the only documentation available for billing that shows that the commercials ran as scheduled. If a station does keep a program log, all of the FCC's logging rules apply to it.

The FCC requires that the log be treated as a legal document. The willful falsification of the log to misrepresent broadcast content *will* cost the station its license, no matter how minor the change may have been. The Commission feels that way about any lie told to it by station personnel; it relies on the candor and honesty of the licensee for self-regulation, and when the Commission finds that a licensee is not trustworthy, it adopts the attitude that the licensee does not have the character qualifications to have a license. Lying to the FCC is thus a "capital offense" for a station.

Of course, mistakes can occur when filling in a log, and when they do, they may be corrected—but only by the person ("operator") who made them. The operator should initial the change to verify that he or she was indeed the one making the correction.

Meter Readings

Except in cases in which the transmitter is monitored automatically in accordance with FCC rules, an operator must be on duty at all times and must periodically take readings on the key meters. Most stations require that these readings be made at least every two hours. They must also be taken when the mode of operation is changed—such as when an AM station changes power or directional antenna pattern at sunset and sunrise—as well as at sign-on and sign-off.

For AM stations, the key readings are plate voltage, plate current, and antenna (or common point) current. In the case of solid-state transmitters, which have no power tubes and thus no plates, I've been told informally by FCC personnel that a power output wattmeter reading may substitute for the first two readings and the indirect-method calculation. For FM stations, the key readings are plate voltage, plate current, and transmitter power output.

Power Output Calculations

The Commission expects operators to be able to calculate the power output of the station from the readings taken because the purpose of the readings is to establish that the power transmitted is within the legal parameters—which are +5 percent and −10 percent of the licensed value. When the inspectors visit a station nowadays, they often ask the on-air operator to do these calculations, and they issue sanctions or fines if the operator can't. Make sure that your people can do them.

There are two ways of calculating AM station power and one for FM stations. The "indirect method" applies to both, so called because you calculate what the output power ought to be based on the electricity that the tubes in the transmitter power-output stage are consuming. That calculation is:

$$\text{Power in Watts} = \text{Plate Voltage} \times \text{Plate Current} \times \text{Efficiency Factor}$$

The efficiency factor is a percentage supplied by the manufacturer of the transmitter, and it should be posted for the reference of the staff. It can be as low as 30 percent (0.30) or as high as 80 percent (0.80), depending on the design of the transmitter.

If the plate voltage is shown in kilovolts (kv), it must be converted to volts, and if the plate current is shown in milliamperes (ma), it must be converted to amperes, or the result of the calculation will not be the correct power in watts. *Kilo* means "times 1,000," so 1.4 kv would be 1,400 volts; *milli* means "divided by 1,000," so 500 ma would be 0.5 amperes.

The other method by which AM station power can be calculated is the "direct method":

Power in Watts = (Antenna Current or Common Point Current)^2 × Antenna Resistance

As you may recall from your school math courses, squaring a number means multiplying it by itself, so the formula can also be written as:

Power in Watts = (Antenna Current × Antenna Current) × Antenna Resistance

Antenna current is called "common point current" when the station uses more than one transmitting tower in order to directionalize its signal. Common point current is the same as antenna current for the purposes of this calculation. Antenna resistance (usually a number under 100 ohms) is found listed on the station license.

An important note: The antenna current reading usually deflects upward when the station modulates (transmits the sound signal); the reading that must be read and logged is an unmodulated value. Logging a modulated antenna current reading almost certainly will be seen by an FCC inspector as a legally binding indication that the station was operating way above its licensed power when it really wasn't. It's unfortunate to get a fine when the station operation was correct, simply because somebody made a mistake on the log.

For FM, only the indirect method formula is used for calculation. The direct method for FM consists of simply reading the power output of the transmitter on its wattmeter.

I asked an FCC engineer how the "indirect method" can be calculated for FM stations using the new generation of solid-state transmitters. These are so new on the market, I find, that the FCC seems to be letting its local field personnel come up with an answer to this on a case-by-case basis. Because reading the wattmeter for transmitter power output is already the "direct method" for FM stations, might reading it satisfy *both* the direct and the indirect power determination for FM transmitters without tubes? The engineer I spoke with conceded that there was currently no official answer to this. The solution, for now, seems to be to check with the engineer in charge of the nearest regional FCC field office, and until a firm rule emerges, handle this in whatever way the engineer advises—and I suggest you try to get it in writing!

Tower Lights

Are there lights on your transmitting tower? If there are, even if the tower is owned by somebody else, your station is responsible for making sure that the lights are operating properly. Although the FCC only requires logging one observation per day of the tower lights (when they are operating correctly), the rules also specify that the operator must take action within a half hour of their failure. This means that the lights should be checked at intervals throughout the hours of darkness, either through direct observation or via a remote control. Violating this rule puts you afoul of not only the FCC, but the Federal Aviation Administration as well.

For that one logged observation per day, I recommend that the tower lights be checked very soon after sunset because if they are going to fail, in my experience the most likely time for it will be just when they are supposed to go on. If they do fail—and a failure of just the top flashing beacon constitutes a reportable failure because it defines the top of the tower for aircraft—the failure must be noted on the operating (or transmitter) log and then reported to the nearest office of the Federal Aviation Administration (FAA).

The telephone number of the FAA location to call should be posted for the airstaff, together with a flashlight so that it can be read and called in the event of a studio power failure that also affects the tower lights. The log entry must be repeated daily until the lights are repaired, and the FAA must be notified whenever the lights are restored to operation.

Contests

The FCC mandate about "licensee candor" means that the design and execution of any station contest must be fair and honest. Stations found to have rigged the outcome of a contest in any way can and will lose their license for it. Making sure that a contest is aboveboard is not hard, and ways of doing that were discussed in Chapter 7. However, I want to reinforce the point that the "player sheets" and other documentation of how the contest was conducted should be saved indefinitely in case a contestant later chooses to complain that he or she was not treated fairly. My suggestion is that you keep that contest information in the station's Public Inspection File.

The Public Inspection File

I believe that the FCC is mistaken in believing that everyone in the community will benefit by having access to the Public Inspection File. As a rule, only competitors, activists, and FCC inspectors ever ask to look at it. Nonetheless, because the Commission considers it a very important part of the licensee's obligations, it is, and that file is an important responsibility of yours—at least part of it is, unless your general manager specifically exempts you.

Meet with your manager and find out to what extent you are responsible for the Public Inspection File. When you find out, obtain a copy of the list of what the FCC expects to be in it. You can get this from the National Association of Broadcasters if your station is a member; if not, ask your station's communications attorney in Washington, D.C. Failing that, obtain it from the nearest FCC regional office.

One of the things that's supposed to be in the Public Inspection File is an FCC booklet explaining the file and listing its contents for the public. The trouble is that last time I checked, the required booklet was printed in the 1970s and was very much out-of-date. Make sure that you do have the booklet in your file, but rely on a more up-to-date list to check the contents for compliance.

Something else that must be in the file is a list of community issues and problems. The program director usually prepares this list. At one time, it had to be compiled by conducting many interviews with community leaders; now it merely requires the good-faith judgment of station management. Nonetheless, it must be thoughtfully and carefully prepared, and I've found it helpful to make it a number-ranked list of the top ten community concerns. This allows you to refer to the previous list and consider how certain concerns have risen or dropped in relative public importance.

This list must be updated every three months, and a copy of it should be given to the general manager and the news director and provided for the reference of the airstaff as well. That's because, as mentioned in Chapter 6, the FCC requires that this list be the basis of public affairs programming during the three-month period during which it's effective, and the station must be able to document that it has indeed addressed on the air at least some of these problems.

Public service announcements (PSAs) can be offered as a means of addressing at least some of these issues, but for them to count, each broadcast must be documented by date, time, and length. Therefore, these PSAs should be on the program log as if they were low-priority commercials so that an "invoice" is prepared and put in the public file to document their use.

Although the FCC now no longer requires any specific percentage or amount of public affairs programming—or of news programming, for that matter—it is very important to have some of each on your schedule to be able to prove to the FCC, if needed, that the station *has* operated in the community interest.

Specifically, public affairs programming consists of a documentary, or a program in which discussion of one or more issues of community significance takes place. The easiest way to handle public affairs programming is to have a weekly discussion program. As mentioned in Chapter 6, this is usually scheduled Sunday morning; this may seem cynical—a way to "bury" the program—but, in fact, I find that listeners usually seem most interested in listening to such programs then.

If your station has a weekly public affairs program, make sure that you provide a form that those who prepare (or run) the show must fill out and return to you to place in the Public Inspection File. The form should document the name of the show, the date it ran, the time it was scheduled, how long it lasted, who the participants were, and what issues were discussed. The community problems list should usually serve as the basis for selecting these topics, although of course any other topic of immediate interest not on that list may also be discussed—and documented for the file! (This includes interviews on deejay shows concerning any such issues, whether planned or spontaneous.)

The Public Inspection File must also include any letters received from the public that either criticize the station's programming or make suggestions for programming, together with the station's response—unless the writer specifically asks that the letter be kept private. In practice, all of the complimentary letters should usually be included, too, to avoid suggesting to readers of the file that you only get complaints.

The letters must be kept on file for only two years—the same length of time required for all station logs (except those relating to Emergency Broadcast System broadcasts and any that apply to an FCC inquiry, which must be retained indefinitely). However, practically speaking, there's no reason not to keep the letters there as long as possible—and to keep the program and transmitter logs indefinitely, too—because these documents might be needed at the next license renewal to prove that the station has operated in a responsible fashion. If someone elects to challenge the station's license at renewal time— seeking the license for themselves by making charges about how the station was operated—it really helps to have hard evidence to refute them.

By the way, at this writing, the FCC is in the process of making major changes in how radio is to alert the public emergencies in the future. Keep up-to-date on equipment and testing requirements because the Commission puts a high priority on having the correct equipment and on accurate and fast response in both test and emergency conditions. Make sure that your staff knows what to do when a disaster of some sort strikes; the station that responds with needed information in times of emergency not only makes points with the FCC but, more importantly, is long remembered gratefully by the public it serves. That's a priceless benefit.

I should mention that the Public Inspection File must be kept at the station's studio or business office—as long as it is located in the city of license or at the transmitter. When the studio or business office is located elsewhere, the matter becomes complicated. The FCC now allows the studio to be located anywhere within the "city grade contour" of the signal, which is the 5 millivolts per meter (mv/m) contour for AM stations and the 3.16 millivolts per meter (mv/m) contour for FM stations, but it wants the Public Inspection File available within the city of license.

If your station is located outside the city of license, check with your communications attorney about how to handle this. You may be advised to establish your Public Inspection File at a public library within the city of license, which would then require that you make regular pilgrimages there to keep the file up-to-date.

Many stations in this situation keep a duplicate file at the studio as well to cover all of the bases. If your station does this, make sure that both files are identical and that both are kept fully up to date.

Because people who ask to see your public file often have an agenda, frequently do not wish the station well, and usually are well aware of the FCC requirements, make sure that all office and on-air personnel know exactly how to handle such requests. (If the file is located in an institution in the city of license, those in charge of it there must clearly and unequivocally be aware of the requirements as well and agree in writing to follow them.)

Specifically, the Public Inspection File must be available to the public, without delay, anytime the station's office (or the office of the institution where the file is kept) is normally open. It must not be locked away during these hours. Those seeking to look at it must be given full access to it and as much time as they need to see it, subject to normal office hours. If they want to make photocopies of anything in the file, they must be allowed to do so using any copier at the site—for which only a normal, competitive per-copy fee may be charged.

However, nobody looking at the file may remove things from it permanently. Therefore, when possible, I feel it is important to have some responsible station person accompany members of the public while they go through the file to make sure that nothing is stolen from it. (If someone were seeking to get the station into trouble, you see, they might steal documents from the file, then report to the FCC that these documents were missing. The station would be hard-pressed to explain why they weren't there.)

Obscenity and Indecency

As the twentieth century ends, the issue of obscenity and indecency on the air has become more and more relevant for programmers. You must understand that the regulations applying to this issue are not a matter of FCC rules but are embodied in federal law, passed by Congress, signed by the President, and tested and upheld by the U.S. Supreme Court. Furthermore, Congress has repeatedly put pressure on the FCC to enforce this law more decisively—under both Republican and Democratic majorities. Don't take it lightly.

The essential point to understand about the federal law prohibiting "obscene or indecent speech, content, or meaning" is that for broadcasting, this means speech, content, or meaning independent of context. Such an interpretation may seem to you to be a violation of the First Amendment—and it would be for a nonbroadcast medium. However, the U.S. Supreme Court has upheld the government's position that because broadcasting is regulated by the government and content is a legitimate criterion in selecting a licensee to use the public airwaves and in determining whether he or she has operated in the "public interest, convenience, and necessity," this restriction to the First Amendment is constitutional as it applies to broadcasting.

In practice, the FCC enforces this law only when a documented complaint is received. The Commission thinks of this law as being somewhat self-regulating and believes that it makes little sense to offend your own listeners—and if they are not offended, they won't complain, thus providing nothing for the Commission to act against. Of course, the problem is that sometimes only a handful of your listeners are offended, and it only takes one complaint to get the FCC involved. Big fines can result.

Use your common sense. Don't program to offend any of your listeners; it really doesn't make good sense for the station as a business, which is what a commercial radio station is. Be sure that your airstaff clearly understands where you draw the line. If one of your on-air people comes to you seeking approval for something that really straddles the line of taste and decency—and if you'd like to permit it— I strongly suggest that you run it by your general manager and let him or her have the final say. It is the manager's job to represent the interests of the owner, and the owner's interests are definitely at risk in a situation like this.

The purpose of this chapter has been to alert you to the reality that, as a program director, you do have specific responsibilities related to protecting the license and to give you some information to help you do it. I must now give the disclaimer that I am not an attorney, and the content of this chapter is simply based on my own experience as a program director, on conversations with FCC inspectors and office personnel, on discussions with communications attorneys and consulting engineers, and on my constant reading of these matters in the trade press. To do your job properly, you should keep up-to-date, through these same methods, on the latest FCC rules and their interpretations and enforcement.

When you ascertain what your responsibilities are concerning the specifics covered in this chapter, get your general manager's permission to direct specific questions about current requirements and interpretations to the station's communications attorney—or to an office of the FCC, if need be. Most general managers will appreciate your professionalism in seeking to take responsibility in programming-related areas for the preservation of the station's license.

13

Attaining Your Career Goals

Identifying Long-Range Personal Goals

For many of us, the pleasure of programming a radio station is satis-faction enough. However, a programmer of fifty-five is a lot less likely to find work easily than one of twenty-five, unless he or she has built quite a reputation. Therefore, it's advisable from the beginning to have some sort of goal in mind for your career. This does not prevent you from taking things as they come and "enjoying the ride," but it does help you go through doors that you may find open and identify when it may be less risky not to seize such opportunities.

Just as it is futile to enter radio broadcasting motivated by a desire to be rich and famous, so it is counterproductive to covet the program director job in hopes of having prestige and more leisure time. If you are just embarking on your career, let me be plain about this. If you hope to become a significant figure in radio programming, you must devote an unhealthy amount of time to the job. Doing the job right requires long hours and endless detail work, and limiting yourself to the hours assigned you is not going to be enough. If you are to please yourself with your work and be judged by what you accomplish, you are going to work many more hours than that. If you are married, I hope you have an understanding and supportive spouse.

One of the chief attractions of the job for those who are suited to it—the endless variety of experiences—is what makes it so time-consuming. It's never boring. If you're not busy constructing a format document, you may be writing and producing an effective spot for the sales department, putting together a presentation tape for the rep firm, coaching a staff member into a better performance on the air, filling in on the air yourself for a sick staff person (in the news department as well as among the on-air personalities), coaxing a recalcitrant piece of control room equipment back into operation, helping your chief engineer with field strength measurements, listening to new music, doing remotes, dreaming up and executing station promotions, keeping track of the competition—and always setting a strong, consistent example for your staff.

Without constant attention to detail, to make sure that everything turns out the way it is supposed to, you will not ultimately be really successful. It all takes a great deal of time. The job also requires an extraordinary commitment—and good judgment on when to compromise and when not to.

Compromise is what brings people together and makes a team work well as a unit. If it's intelligent compromise, it can result in win-win situations in which the ultimate product reaching the consumer, the programming, does not become burdened with incomprehensible contradictions. If a compromise will damage that product, another solution must be found.

An acquaintance of mine, the late programmer Rick Carroll, is best remembered for two stunning successes: the first FM Top 40 station to beat an AM Top 40 in Los Angeles, KKDJ, in the early seventies, and considerably later the Modern Rock format that turned KROQ (FM), a perennial loser in Los Angeles radio, into a nationally copied success. What is often forgotten is that his previous attempts to program album rock hybrid formats on what were supposed to be Top 40 stations were never particularly successful. There are several lessons to be learned from this.

The first lesson is that without taking risks, you cannot succeed. No risk, no gain. If you do what everybody else is doing, any success you realize will be attributed to others, and only your failures will be attributed to you. Carroll always took risks for what he believed was right.

The second lesson is to understand how the audience perceives the station. Carroll had difficulty doing that. Like many visionary programmers, he was way ahead of the audience much of the time, and that cost him. Only when Rick reevaluated his thinking and developed stations that would appeal to the audiences then available did he achieve the spectacular successes, which have eclipsed his failures.

The third lesson is that you must be committed to the vision you develop. Hear the station in your head, put it all down on paper for your staff (rationale as well as procedure), and execute it the way it should be done. The station may well sound unconventional, and many people working with you will be uncomfortable with that and will urge changes to make the station sound more like others, but if you compromise your vision, it won't work, and you'll eventually be taking the blame for that.

The fourth lesson is to learn from experience. Know your strengths and weaknesses. Try to develop your thinking along the lines of the people to whom you're programming. Remember what I told you about major-market Adult Contemporary programmer Bobby Irwin back in Chapter 5!

The fifth lesson is to plan everything on the air for listener effect, rather than to observe conventional radio procedure. When you work backward from your goals and objectives, the best means of achieving them becomes much clearer—and often turns out to be less expensive to do than "the normal way."

Here's the final lesson: Rick Carroll was perhaps *too* uncompromising at times. He eventually lost most of his jobs by being rather rigidly inflexible with management and thus seeming to have a different agenda than they did (they were hoping to make money and have a successful business). Be diplomatic, and work to gain management's confidence that your concept will be successful and profitable. You won't be permitted to do what you know must be done without the approval and support of the station's management and ownership. However, the other side of the coin is that you can't take the risks you need to take to develop your career if you are petrified about the possibility of losing your job.

Nobody likes to be fired, and few people really like quitting over principle (which is probably less wise than letting yourself be fired because you can't collect unemployment benefits if you resign). However, if you aren't willing to risk being fired for what you are certain is right—however reluctantly—then you will eventually retreat from what you know is the right thing to do. You will accept destructive compromises, and your budding career will disappear with the ratings—and you may eventually get fired anyway. No risk, no potential for gain.

If you do have a clear vision of your audience and what will please it, if you do succeed in constructing consistent programming to achieve your vision, and if you do show such commitment to it that your staff goes ahead and executes it properly despite their impulse to want to "do it the way everybody else does", then you have the makings of one of those few programmers who eventually become well known throughout the business.

That reputation may help you still get programming jobs at age fifty-five or, perhaps more likely, will make possible a consulting career in your later years. Consulting sounds like fun, but it does require a good reputation, clients, cash flow, and a lot of time for the business to develop—or it too easily becomes unpaid idleness, leading eventually back to some programming job somewhere.

Mandatory: A Savings Plan

You won't accomplish anything in this business without a willingness to take risks, starting with the risk of losing your job. That takes money; some savings. At this point, you are probably laughing hollowly, agreeing that would be a good idea if only there were a dime or two left over after you pay the bills. Nonetheless, you must get a nest egg going somehow, or else you'll never dare to risk your job and you will never get where you need to go.

Here are a few strategies. First and foremost, if you can arrange to have the accounting department subtract a fixed amount from every paycheck for your savings, do it. It's a lot harder to save money after you get your hands on it. If possible, have the accountant deposit that amount directly into a special account for you—a credit union or a bank account that you don't use for daily expenses or, better yet, a mutual fund—a fund that invests in the stock market.

There are a couple of very good reasons to use a mutual fund for savings. One reason is that your money will grow a lot faster over time in a mutual fund than through conventional interest-bearing savings accounts, although it will be subject to gains and losses from day to day based on market fluctuations. If that bothers you, the solution is simply not to follow your fund's value in the daily newspaper. Some years are better than others in the stock market, but, over decades, the compounded annual gain has been around 10 percent for most of the twentieth century, beating any other form of investment over the long haul.

The other good reason for using a mutual fund is that the money is available if you need it, but not *easily* available. It takes a few days and a little work to get it. This helps prevent frivolous use of this vital nest egg.

Bear in mind that I am relating my own findings and experiences here. I am no more qualified as a financial advisor than I am as a lawyer. With that warning, here are a few of my own opinions on how to select an appropriate mutual fund.

First, the fund you select must invest mostly in stocks—equities—if it is to grow as you want it to. You can use an annual listing, such as the *Forbes* "Honor Roll of Mutual Funds," or daily "grades," such as those printed in the mutual fund section of the *Investor's Business Daily* newspaper, to find the best-performing funds over a long period of time.

If you are more conservative with your money, use a fund indexed to the Standard and Poors 500. Your fund will never outperform the stock market, but it will never underperform it either, and indexed funds have indeed outperformed the majority of standard stock funds over the long haul and also have lower annual costs to subtract from the fund shares.

Unless you have a chunk of change to start out with, look at the mutual fund families that permit you to open an account with a small amount of money and that encourage you to add a small amount with each regular investment. Janus and Twentieth Century are two companies that come to mind; undoubtedly there are others. When you have opened the account, dedicate a specific amount from each paycheck for deposit—directly deposited by your station if possible. If necessary, though, be ready to write and mail the check yourself.

Explore the subject further, if you're interested. It's your money, and investing can be fun.

Once you have a savings plan set up, every time you get a raise, increase your withheld savings amount by most if not all of the difference. If you can avoid the temptation to embellish your lifestyle with each raise, you'll save a lot of money and be better insulated against financial disaster when you get fired. (Everybody in the business gets fired eventually. Don't take it personally.)

Also, if you have access to a retirement plan—particularly one that invests in the stock market—take advantage of it. If your company will match your contribution up to a specific amount, do all you can to contribute at least that much. Even though you won't get your hands on it for years, it is your money, and you just can't lose when the company doubles your contribution. (If you leave the job, roll over that money into a tax-sheltered investment—such as an individual retirement account—to avoid paying taxes and penalties on it, and worse yet, spending it.)

Set up a permanent ledger when you open your fund account, and record the date and amount of every additional investment you make. Although you will pay taxes on your received dividends and distributed capital gains annually as they are paid to you, you have one more tax concern that you must prepare for from the beginning: when you sell any of your shares, you must report the capital gain or loss on each share you sell—the difference between what you paid for it and what you sold it for.

Thus you need to know what you paid for each share to satisfy the Internal Revenue Service. This is very difficult if you haven't kept records from the beginning, and it's very easy if you have. Just figure that the first share you bought is the first you sold, and so on, every time you need to sell shares to raise cash, and the matter takes care of itself.

Many funds pay out gains, particularly in January of each year, to keep the share price in a particular range, but you must still show on your annual tax return the purchase and sale price and dates for each share when you sell. I recommend that you have the dividends you receive reinvested automatically. If you do, you must keep a record of these purchases and the price at which they were purchased because you'll have to know your capital gain on these in whatever year you eventually sell them.

Planning for the Future

Building your savings helps insulate you against job loss. For many programmers, though, the ultimate goal is not just getting to be a better-known program director and not just having less to worry about if they lose their job, but getting into a position where they have more security or responsibility in management—or perhaps getting into ownership and being their own boss. Let's look at a couple of options.

General Manager Job

Do you want to be a general manager? It means having the responsibility for the overall billing of the station and for its success as a business. Do you want to tackle that? It means being the leader of every department, including sales, instead of just programming. Are you up to that?

If you are, good for you. It won't be easy. As I mentioned previously, general managers are usually drawn from sales because they have ultimate responsibility for the station's financial success as a business. (General managers often receive an "override" of perhaps 1.5 to 3 percent on the total gross billing of the station. In return, they receive no standard commission for any selling they may personally do.)

This means that you'll need to gain some knowledge and expertise in sales. If you attend sales meetings as I have suggested, you're making a start. Go farther and volunteer to make client calls with the salespeople. Watch not only what they do, but what they don't do, in dealing with the client. You may discover that you know how to give clients better service and write better advertising than the salespeople do. Volunteer to help write spots and even prepare sales presentations for the salespeople from time to time.

When you are ready to give it a try, sit down with the general manager and indicate that you have aspirations to gain sales experience for an eventual managerial position and would like to handle a few accounts for no commission—just to pay some dues and gain some experience. Some program directors have left programming to go into sales as "general manager training," but this can be a really bad idea. It reduces your rank in management, and it may not be as fulfilling as your previous job—meaning that you may not do it as well as you should. This can actually reduce your chances of making manager in the long run.

Instead, I suggest that you add whatever sales activities you can while keeping your programming job. You'll demonstrate competence, capacity, and versatility—which are the attributes of a general manager! If there is no managerial opportunity at your station, this experience will be helpful in working toward such an opportunity elsewhere.

Station Ownership

How about ownership? At some time or other, every program director covets the idea of programming his or her own radio station. If you find yourself thinking about this quite a bit, maybe you should be taking the dream seriously.

Unless you have an inheritance, you are unlikely to be able to save up enough money from your program director's salary to bring this dream to life yourself. This means that you'll have to interest others in your goal—others who have money, who would like to invest it in a radio station, and who see your expertise as the key to making it pay off as a business. (Your involvement in service clubs and civic activities, as suggested earlier, may be helpful in making such contacts.)

Your share of ownership may be arranged as "sweat equity"— paid for by your own expertise and work—but make sure you get at least a living wage, too. Do not fail to get your equity share guaranteed in writing. Even trusted friends and family members may go back on their word later on, or may remember the agreement differently than you do. Don't take the chance.

If you are to bring this particular dream to a successful conclusion, you must be more than just the "programming guru." You must get involved in all aspects of planning the station as a business because most nonradio investors have no clear idea of what makes radio profitable. Investors often think it should be easy to make a profit because radio is labor intensive. That is, it costs about the same to run a station that has no commercials as it does to run a station that is sold out, meaning that after paying the overhead and reaching the break-even point, everything else netted is largely profit. With your programming expertise, investors may assume, how can they lose?

This sort of thinking is very dangerous and leads to many catastrophic failures. It does make it easier to gain investors, and it's true as far as it goes, but the big problem is *reaching* that break-even point, and the number one problem in situations like this is under-capitalization. It does cost money to run a station—more than investors may think—and if the station doesn't make that much back in the monthly billing, any accumulating red ink can rapidly destroy the station.

Make sure that your investors know that they must be prepared to bankroll the station with no revenue at all for at least a year. Get their commitment to make up any deficits for a minimum of two years. Most likely there will be some billing pretty quickly, so investors probably won't have to shovel in as much cash as this obligates them for, but it is not at all uncommon to find a new station or ownership running a deficit for at least two years.

Go over the budgeting with your investors. Make realistic estimates of all costs. In fact, estimate high. It's tempting to low-ball everything to gain investors' approval, but they probably aren't likely to pull out at this point if you are realistic. At any rate, it's best that investors pull out now before realism becomes reality than bail out on you when the losses exceed what you'd projected. If you get their approval for realistic-to-high budgeting, what actually happens should be well accepted by your backers. If you come in under budget, you will have greatly strengthened your investors' confidence in you.

In your budgeting, make sure that every category is covered, including any needed engineering upgrades, if it's an existing station, and generous construction costs if it's a new one. Two categories that I've seen overlooked, thus throwing off a critical budget and eventually causing much financial misery, are the withholding (payroll) taxes and the music license fees. Make sure that you cover everything in your planning.

Regardless of what your career goals may be right now, be flexible. Goals change; unexpected opportunities arise. Be versatile. Get that sales experience I mentioned. Learn all aspects of station operation, and, especially, be the most dedicated, intuitive, detail-oriented program director you can be. It will pay off for you again and again in your career.

Good luck to you!

Index

CPSIA information can be obtained at www.ICGtesting.com
Printed in the USA
LVOW07s0309071213

364226LV00003B/97/A